T0065422

REFLECTIONS

Uplifting and inspiring true stories
of family, faith, and life

Colleen Loran &
Christine Heath

WESTBOW
PRESS*
A DIVISION OF THOMAS NELSON
& ZONDERVAN

This book is a work of non-fiction. Unless otherwise noted, the author and the publisher make no explicit guarantees as to the accuracy of the information contained in this book and in some cases, names of people and places have been altered to protect their privacy.

WestBow Press books may be ordered through booksellers or by contacting:

WestBow Press
A Division of Thomas Nelson & Zondervan
1663 Liberty Drive
Bloomington, IN 47403
www.westbowpress.com
844-714-3454

Scripture taken from the King James Version of the Bible.

ISBN: 978-1-6642-1588-7 (sc)
ISBN: 978-1-6642-1589-4 (e)

Print information available on the last page.

WestBow Press rev. date: 01/20/2021

Introduction

THIS IS A COMPOSITE OF WRITINGS THAT MY IDENTICAL, TWIN sister, Colleen created throughout her life. I found them in her journals and notebooks after her unexpected passing. She expressed herself in her writings and my goal is to get these inspiring stories in print, so that others could share in her memories.

Dedication

THIS BOOK OF WRITINGS IS DEDICATED TO HER CHILDREN: ALAN, John, Daniel, and Christina. These children were her most precious treasures and dedicated to our Lord Jesus Christ who she loved and faithfully served.

Left to right: Alan, Daniel, John, Colleen, & Christina

John, Daniel, Alan, & Christina at Colleen's
Memorial Service October 2019

Preface

THROUGH THE YEARS, EVER SINCE HIGH SCHOOL, MY SISTER Colleen loved to write. She wrote all kinds of things, poems, thoughts, reflections etc. She even tried to publish a few in different magazines and a newspaper. She also joined writers' clubs, book clubs and took some writing courses. At one of her memorial services in Athens, Georgia, a friend of hers, Beverly, a publisher and author, came up to me with tears in her eyes said, "I've seen some of her writings, you should get them published. She was very good; she was able to write heartfelt stories of her family and life. She never wanted to be famous or well-known, but she wrote for her family to know about her."

Colleen was never able to fulfill her dream. Some of her stories our mom and I have heard and read over the years; some are new to us. As I went through her notebooks, journals and papers, I chose some of the best. I wanted to give her this in her memory.

In loving memory of
Colleen Joy Loran
February 10, 1955 to September 27, 2019
from her twin sister Christine Heath
and mother Bessie Yarrington.

Christine & Colleen - December 15, 2017

Acknowledgement

I WOULD LIKE TO THANK MY FAMILY FOR ALL THEIR SUPPORT AND help in completing this book. Compiling Colleen's notes and journals was a task I needed some advice on. My mom, Bessie Yarrington who from the beginning thought with me that this book should be written, and helped me with proofreading and what to include. To Rebekah Barr, my daughter, who was so helpful with computer technicalities. To Jeremy Baker, my son-in-law who helped proofread.

Stand in Awe

by Colleen Joy Loran
A book about a life restored by God's promises

*******Christines notes: Colleen had this page all written before I started this project. It's amazing to me how she had everything planned.*

DEDICATION

THIS BOOK IS DEDICATED TO OUR LORD JESUS CHRIST WITHOUT WHOM there would be no story to write. All the credits for this work go to my Lord and Savior Jesus Christ without whom I would have nothing noteworthy to say. And to my heavenly Father, creator of this gorgeous earth and all the beauty in nature that inspires me so and who created me and saved me from birth, and to the Holy Spirit who comforts, strengthens, guides and directs my life and anoints me to write above my natural abilities. All glory and honor and praise go to the three in one!

4/30/04 Psalms 44 :8. In my Bible I wrote: I want to write stories that bring people hope. Because he has given us so much, let us return to him a life of worship, a song of joy, a prayer of thanksgiving, and a heart of love.

3/10/02 Psalm 42 "As the deer pants for streams of water, so my soul pants for you, oh God. My soul thirsts for God, for the living God. When can I go and meet with God?"

Psalms 42:5b, 8 "Put your hope in God for I will yet praise Him, my Savior and my God." "by day the Lord directs His love and at night his song is with me."

Psalm 63 "A prayer to God of my life."

Song *You Deserve the Glory*

You deserve the glory and the honor.
Lord, we lift our hands in worship,
As we lift Your holy name.
You deserve the glory and the honor.
Lord, we lift our hands in worship,
As we lift Your holy name.
You are great;
You do miracles so great.
There is no one else like You.
There is no one else like You.
You are great;
You do miracles so great.
There is no one else like You.
There is no one else like You.

Thanks

TO THE MANY PEOPLE, FAMILY AND FRIENDS WHO HAVE PRAYED, supported and encouraged me and for my children.

I thank God for each of you. So many times, I desperately needed you to hold my arms up when I was so burdened, discouraged, lonely, hurting and weary. Thank you for not giving up on me.

******Christine's notes: I found this included in Colleens' notes.

Foreword

My dreams for my life. Written 2/15/ 2010 Age 55

To write an inspiring book about all the trials and joys and what God has done. The awesome things God has shown and taught me about his ways.

To encourage and inspire all those who would read any part of it, to put their lives in God's hands. "Call unto Me and I will thee answer, and show thee great and mighty things which thou knowest not." Jeremiah 33:3

As I prayed, I felt an impression from the Lord: maybe things will start to happen and He will answer you. For my children to know how God answered prayer in my life.

Deuteronomy 6:5-9 says "You should love the Lord your God with all your heart, your soul and with all your strength. And these words which I command you today shall be in your heart, you should teach them diligently to your children and shall talk of them when you sit in your house, when you walk by the way, and when you lie down and when you rise up. you should bind them as a sign on your hand, and they shall be frontlets between your eyes, and you should write them on the door post of your house and on your gates."

To write down these things for the children. Just as you would write in a baby book all the cute things, so you will never forget those precious moments, because as humans we do forget. The Israelites forgot the powerful and mighty acts of God in their lives and the lives of their fathers and grandfathers. This is for my children and grandchildren. These are all the reasons that I write.

"When all that generation has been gathered to their fathers, another generation arose after them, who did not know the Lord, nor the work which he had done for Israel" Judges 2:10

*******Christine's notes: The following was written by John, Colleen's middle son, as a eulogy for her memorial service in Brooksville Florida.*

Mom loved waterfalls; she did her entire life. She would talk of the "creek", where she grew up. She had pictures in her house in Athens, GA, of waterfalls, books about waterfalls, magazines, postcards etc. I think for her they helped her feel peaceful, they felt like home. I think waterfalls have a spirit of purity, of cleansing.

I have so many memories of waterfalls with mom. In the Finger Lakes region of central NY, we would visit Treman, Taughannock, Buttermilk, Watkins Glen, Pratt Falls, Cazenovia Falls, and Tinker Falls. The list goes on. Throughout my life I have been drawn to creeks and waterfalls.

I think they mean to me, all the same things that I imagine they meant to her. A place in time, of peace and beauty, of cleansing and healing. A place to see God; but waterfalls have another storm under the surface. While they are beautiful, they are also rugged and often in remote and hard to reach places. Streams converge and erode the soil and stone. Only after ages of time and pressure the beauty stands to form.

For me, I think the waterfall will be a way to remember mom, to remember things that were beautiful. But I think also they point out that in the beauty there is also struggle. In each of us there is beauty, and there's struggle. I think the acknowledgment of both gets us closer to the truth, when we see each other in this way. When I see mom in this way, I can see myself, the beauty and struggle. I will always remember the beauty and I hope to remember that beauty and struggle are interwoven. I hope that perspective will encourage me toward empathy and grace and to see that in everyone.

Colleen with Daniel & Alan

The Miracle Babies

By Colleen Joy Loran

"Miracle babies" that's what they called us. The doctors, nurses, and staff at the small-town hospital in Gloversville, New York. An upstate town named for the glove factory there. Over the course of my life, my mother has recounted to me on numerous occasions the miraculous events surrounding my birth. I felt that after almost 50 years I should share this story with others, to give God the glory He deserves.

It was February 1955. A winter icy storm had moved in. My mother, who was 7 Months pregnant, fell on the ice and snow while going to the mailbox from her parents' rural home in upstate N.Y. She was rushed to her doctor (Dr. McMartin), and then to the hospital. The doctor scheduled x-rays and an emergency c-section. (Dr. Kaiser, who was a specialist, did the surgery.) My Mom had high blood pressure, which led to toxemia, and her kidneys had collapsed. The x-rays revealed two tiny, premature twins, who were in great danger. The baby girls were delivered in the middle of the afternoon. The first and stronger of the two was named Christine Joan. She was 3 pounds and 13 ounces. Three minutes later I was born, weighing 2 pounds 13 ounces. I was named Colleen Joy.

Due to the lack of oxygen we were black and blue all over, and very frail. The small rural hospital in Gloversville N.Y. had only one incubator, and no neonatal unit. They did all they could for Christine, leaving me to the side, believing that there was no hope. Because of our poor condition and appearance, they didn't let my mother see us, not wanting to put more stress on her already weakened condition. She was not expected to survive the day. The Red Cross notified my father who was on a ship in the middle of the Mediterranean Sea. He was in the Navy. They were to pick him up in a helicopter and bring him home to attend three funerals, not expecting either one of us or our Mother to survive.

My mother's father (My Grandfather) had been with my mom (who was his youngest daughter) the whole time. My Mom had been staying with my Grandparents during her pregnancy while my father was away. My Grandfather, whose name was Howard G. Young, was a quiet man with a lot of faith in a powerful God. You see 18 years prior when his daughter (my mother), was only eighteen months old, his wife died of kidney disease (toxemia poison), leaving him heartbroken with four small children. He had seen hard times before and God had brought him through. His silent prayers were being heard in heaven.

A nurse by the name of Mrs. Smit went over to check me and discovered that I was still alive! In the meantime, they put me in the incubator with my sister, and I immediately begin to respond. They sent for another incubator. The doctor was amazed that I was still living; but did not want my mother to have false hopes that I would survive. All three of us were still in grave condition. My grandfather went home and stayed on his knees throughout the night praying for a miracle. The small Free Methodist Church where he worshiped held an-all-night prayer vigil.

The next morning the doctors said that it was a miracle we lasted through the night. The doctors feared that even if we did survive, we would have numerous health problems, and brain damage, particularly me, since they had left me for so long without any care. Each day and night the doctors believed would be our last. But my Grandfather's prayers sustained us. Each and every day we grew stronger, as did my mother. After a week they finally did let my mother see us.

We did survive and finally my Mother was able to go home. Six weeks later, Christine was allowed to go home. The doctor cautioned my mother that she would not survive the first cold or sickness of any kind. The day finally came when I would go home. That day there was a huge snowstorm in Upstate N.Y. and the roads were not passable. My Mother walked a mile down the country road to the nearest phone at a neighbor's, to call the hospital to say she wanted to come to get her baby, but because of the condition of the roads, she would not be able to.

Finally, my Mother was able to come and take me home. The doctor still warned her that the slightest illness could take her babies. She took very good care of us. Even though she had no nurses training, and no prior experience with babies (She was a brand-new mother) she had God's strength and guidance, and a strong Mother's instinct. She took excellent care of us and we not only survived, but thrived.

My Mother slept downstairs in the living room with the only source of heat, a wood burning stove. She slept with one baby lying on each shoulder on her chest. She was constantly afraid the wood stove would go out in the night and we would catch pneumonia from the chill.

*******Christine's notes: My mother told how we were on different formulas, and had to be fed every two hours. The refrigerator they had, at the time, had a icebox in the middle, so as to not mix them up, she put one set of formulas on one side and one on the other. Also, they just had a ringer washer. She said she washed 90 diapers a week and put them on the clothesline out in the frigid air. They came in frozen stiff, partially dry, and then she finished drying them on racks near the wood stove. My grandparents and our uncle all helped my mom with the care of the little twins.*

When we were about nine months, old my grandmother had shingles. They didn't know at the time that people could get chicken pox from shingles. My sister and I both came down with a severe case of chicken pox. The high fever resulted in Christine having convulsions and she developed a heart murmur. We were both extremely ill but with a lot more tender and loving care and prayer we survived again.

The pediatrician was amazed and thrilled to see us at our first-year checkup. He confessed to my Mother that he never expected to see us again, feeling that we would never live to see our first birthday. From that day till now, almost 50 years later, Christine and I have grown up normal and healthy with no chronic or debilitating conditions of any kind. We have been blessed with excellent health.

As we were growing up our Mother made sure we always got our rest and ate a healthy diet. We rarely took any medicine, and she taught us how extremely important it was to take good care of ourselves. I went on to nursing school, got married and had four healthy children naturally, with no drugs or surgery. In fact, the only time I have ever been in the hospital was to give birth to each of my four children.

My first son was so strong and healthy he was born weighing in at 10 pounds, 2 ounces! My mom came to the hospital to see her first grandchild, whose mother had been the younger, smaller, weaker twin. The one that had been left aside to die by the hospital staff because they felt I would have severe brain damage and many physical challenges. Remembering how tiny I was and then seeing how I had delivered a ten-pound son naturally, with no drugs or complications, was truly miraculous to her. Praise be to God.

"For you created my inmost being; you knit me together in my Mother's womb. I praise you because I am fearfully made; your works are wonderful, I know that full well...When I was woven together in the depths of the earth, Your eyes saw my unformed body. All the days ordained for me were written in your book before one of them came to be. How precious to me are your thoughts O

God! How vast is the sum of them. Were I to count them they would outnumber the grains of sand." Psalms 139:13-17

Baby twins with Grandpa and Grandma Young and uncle Harvey.

*******Christine's notes: Colleen wrote this first entry, while living in*
Tully, NY

Memories

Memories of my childhood are very sweet and pleasant; carefree summers are mostly what I think of. The creek down in the woods behind our home, or Grandpa's house, both places out in the country. I do so love the quiet countryside, no traffic or noise, just the symphony of God's creation! Birds chirping and singing, sweet melodies of praise to God, who cares for them. To this day I love my windows and doors open to the morning, cool air; hearing all the blessed sounds of nature.

Summertime Memories

The old door was very familiar, with its big glass window and heavy oak wood. I smiled to myself as I unhooked the latch and opened the door. My heart skipped a beat and my elation knew no bounds, as I stepped out into the sweet fragrance of the fresh, morning air and brilliant sunlight.

The warmth of the sun on my face drew me off the porch and into the yard. The peaceful atmosphere and exquisite beauty enhanced with each passing moment. The lush green grass and magnificent maple trees; underneath a sapphire sky captivated my attention. My being drank in the picturesque scene that encompassed me. It seemed that if I could atone each moment, that it would last a Lifetime! The meadowlands, robin, and cardinals, were singing a melodious psalm. A miniature bubbling brook gurgled and danced over the rocks between its grassy banks; then ran alongside the treelined, paved lane.

On the other side of the road was a notched fence; probably built by Indians, long ago, for which the road was named. It remained unmoved and solid. Each huge stone supporting another. So perfect for this natural setting; of a natural simple life. The serene yard of my grandfather's homestead has always left me in a state of euphoria. How I loved it here!

So quiet. No sounds at all except for nature's tranquil symphony, erasing any of the unpleasant things, in life; soothing any hurts, comforting any pain, calming all my fears and encouraging me to forget any disappointments. Nature's sanctuary, where you could meet God. His Holy presence was everywhere. A Line of a poem my Mother had read to me floated into my memory. "One is nearer to God's heart, in a garden, than anywhere else on earth!"

My thoughts quieted as I gazed at the old wooden rope swing, in the center of the yard, under the majestic maple tree. It seemed to beckon me as it swayed gently in the soft breeze. I ran and jumped onto the seat and it carried me higher and higher until my toes touched the leaves. I felt intoxicated by the warmth of the sun and the sweet fresh scent of hay and honey suckle. Leaning way back in the swing, I watched the puffy, white, cotton clouds drift across the glassy, blue sky.

Across the way was a large meadow. Cozy and inviting with its yellow buttercups, purple cornflowers, white daises, orange tiger lilies and ivory Queen Anne's Lace. Grandfather's yard also yielded a variety of blossoms. White and violet, lilac bushes, white morning glories, light pink, fuchsia and red hollyhocks, decorated the side of the modest, white, framed house. I had two long weeks to bask in this solitude. The pleasure of knowing how much my grandfather adored me, completed my joy.

Colleen on swing at grandpa Young's
home at Indian Rd. Fonda, NY

On Hammocks

I'm convinced that everyone should have a hammock in their yard. To lie in a hammock and look up at the sky through the beautiful green leaves of the tree that suspends you in a piece of heaven. The gentle sway reminds you of being carried when you were little. The peace and serenity transports the burdens of your soul to another place, where no pain and trouble are. The expanse of the big blue sky, and the towering trees remind you that God is in heaven and all is well in the world, because he is in control!

Whether it's a quick 15 minutes or a luxurious hour and a nap, you feel refreshed like you've been away on a relaxing vacation. The blessings of a hammock just outside my front door, beckons me to come away and talk to my Heavenly Father or just bask in the sunshine of His love!

"The earth is the Lord's and the fullness thereof." He put man in a garden as a caretaker, we are His temple. I have always been a lover of nature.

My parents bought a piece of property from the Forbes's. A farm outside of Cortland, NY. The property was on a hillside overlooking a valley. As a young girl I just adored being outside. Listening to God's sweet symphony of birds and insects, the quiet of the woods, down in back of our home and the creek down deep into the woods. The creek was beautiful, and had big flat rocks over which the water would flow. Just below where we used a trail to get down through the woods to get to our creek, there were high rock walls and a small gorge emerged. It was breathtaking. The smell of the wet vegetation, that fresh earthy smell of moss, so refreshing, like a thunderstorm had just drenched the earth. That fresh smell after a good hard rain, was always in the woods because of the ever-running source of water.

One Sunday we tried to follow the creek up stream. We walked and walked and never did find the source. I would love to have the opportunity to go back and try it again, maybe with my grown son who had his CPR and red cross training as a life guard. I'm not as young as I used to be.

We are to be good stewards of all He has given us. When did we stop being caretakers of the earth? After the fall, after man was banned from the garden of Eden? When did mankind start polluting, being careless and negligent? Every time we pollute creation we are cursed, we get sick, and diseased. It is a circle that will come back to bite us. As Christians we are all called to be caretakers of the earth.

The Beauty of a Garden

The more dark, and evil the world becomes, the more beauty we need to compensate. Beauty of all created things, it's not a luxury, but a necessity for us to behold and believe that God loves us and has a better life and future for us. Beauty and joy bring light and life into an otherwise drab and meaningless existence. Beauty of nature can inspire us like nothing else can. It inspires us to worship God freely with abandon. I love the song, "You make beautiful things out of my life".

Seasons

What season do you like best? I've often been asked that. Well, that depends on where you are geographically. In the north, I love summer best of all. In the south, I love spring time best. The worst would be no seasons. The north has long, cloudy, gray, winter days. In the south, there is a long, hot, dry summer. I thought one time it wouldn't be too bad if the seasons of your life went by as fast as the seasons of the year. In three months, you would know that a trial or difficulty would end; that wouldn't be too bad, instead of going through it year after year. However, if you were at a particularly good time in your life, it might have to end in only three months; that's way too soon for a good time in life to end.

We must put the seasons of our lives into Gods' hands and trust his perfect timing for the seasons, good or bad to come and go. Psalm 91:14-16. Contentment with godliness, is great gain. Paul said it in 1st Timothy 6:6.

What I Liked, Growing Up

Reading: Mysteries – *Nancy Drew*, and books about girls who went to Nursing School. *Island of the Blue Dolphin*. The creek, the meadow. Kickball, Toboggan – sledding downhill (sledding to the bus stop on Forbes Rd). Playing dress up at Grandpa's house. (I was head mistress of Grandpa's house for 2 weeks. I cooked and cleaned, played outside and loved it). Camping and water skiing. Word of

Reflections

Life Camp – The Island at Schroon Lake NY. Being identical twins. Game – *Clue*.

Remembering the time Chris and I and Mark went down to the creek in the winter time. Mark fell in. We undressed him, taking off his wet clothes, and put our dry clothes on him. He never caught a cold, and mom didn't know!

Old-Fashioned Girl

I am an old fashioned girl, a bit of a dreamer. I like antiques, and beautiful old Victorian houses, fireplaces, history, calligraphy writing, heirlooms, old pictures, scrap booking, and letters, not emails. Tea parties, pastels, flowers, hammocks, and swings. Country meadows, views of the sky and horizon, leisurely walks, baking and cooking, taking care of one's own home and children. Natural childbirth, breast-feeding, making your own baby food, gardening, essential oils, recycling, anything natural and good for you. Courtship, romance, gentlemen and ladies. I love nature, walking outside, and waterfalls.

Seek Ye First

"The blessing of the LORD it maketh rich, and He addeth no sorrow with it" Proverbs 10:22 Gods' way = no sorrow. Our way = curses.

I love to hear from my children, cards, letters, phone calls, e-mails, and visits. Their love and affection are so sweet and dear to me. I love the tender love care and affection of my husband. Compliments, touches, any consideration at all. I loved to be loved, period!

When I think of others, many do all kinds of things, good and bad to get approval from peers, friends, parents, children etc. Where do we get this from? This need to be loved? Craving to be appreciated? I believe in the purest form it comes from God. He desires our love, adoration, praise, and gratitude. He goes to all lengths to convey His love to us. Sunrises, sunsets, beauty of nature, even sacrificing His only Son, just to have a relationship with us!

I love to look at the sky! "Of old hast thou laid the foundation of the earth: and the heavens are the work of thy hands. They shall perish, but thou shalt endure: yea, all of them shall wax old like a garment; as a vesture shalt thou change them, and they shall be changed: But thou art the same, and thy years shall have no end." Psalm 102:25-27

A Pastor's Wife.

I had no idea what a pastor's wife was supposed to do, when I became one at the ripe young age of 21. I had also just started nursing school the same month we moved into the parsonage, in Auburn, New York! After giving it a lot of thought and prayer, I decided that a Christian wife and eventually a mother, was the best way to also be the Pastors' Wife. That was my plan, my goal in life and I set out with God's help to do just that.

Getting Ready for Babies

My son's father and I had been married for 5 years. When I found out I was pregnant for the first time, I was so happy I cried! I found out over the phone. I had taken my sample to a health clinic and they called me with the news!

We were living in Auburn NY in the parsonage, a big rambling old white house in town on Seymour St. Yes, I was a pastor's wife at our first church. The church was a small white church, the people were wonderful! I had fixed up the nursery at the church for any babies that happened to come. I could now fix up a nursery at home! That was so much fun.

Reflections

Upstairs in that big old house were 4 rooms, freshly painted. I chose the yellow room for the nursery. I made gingham curtains, and found a white, second hand crib at a yard sale. I found 2 dressers at my mom's, a small white chest of drawers, and a low table dresser with one big drawer and 2 shelves underneath. I painted both white, and painted the knobs different pastel colors. I bought a pad for the top of the low one to use for the dressing table, as it had lots of storage underneath. I also painted a rocking chair white, and trimmed it in yellow and green. I made cushions and pillows with the green and yellow gingham I had made the curtains out of. My mom gave me a beautiful, yellow and white lamb mobile that I used for each child. I later sent it to Dan and Karen for my first grandson, Noah, and it still worked! I lined the drawers and both shelves with baby paper from the gifts I received from the 5 baby showers given to me!

After the church shower, my mom gave me one after Alan was born to so that the baby could meet friends and relatives. Jackie Banner gave Chris and I one together, a twin's shower (Not planning it, we both became pregnant with in 3 months of each other.) My mother-in-law gave me a shower also. I bought flannel material and made diapers for my first baby. They were so cute and soft. I had found cut-out plywood animals in the basement of the house, so I painted them and put them in the nursery along with a stuffed dog nursery lamp that had been in the family. I gained 60lbs (craved prime rib)!

Chris made me a beautiful baby quilt with pastel gingham colors and animals. I still have it! Mom bought me a wooden cradle, that each child in our family has used to sleep in. Andrea also used it for her 3 girls. Noah was in San Deigo, CA when he was born, so he didn't use it. My first baby gift was a luxurious, silk baby pillow and quilt from Al's mother and sister.

I always wanted to be a wife and have children. It was my dream. I always wanted four children like my mom had, although no twins! I loved being a twin, but I just wanted one baby at a time. I figured

I would have a mixture of sons and daughters. I never gave much thought about gender, just a mixture. After 3 sons, I had doubts about ever having a daughter and grieved over that for years, but God had his reasons, and they were good ones.

Being a mom was my true calling! I knew from a very young age I would be a full time mom and that I would nurse all of my babies. My conviction to have them all with natural childbirth, with no drugs came later, probably during my nursing school education. My 3 sons are my pride, and my daughter is my joy. I was able to have each of them by natural childbirth and nurse each of them. I also stayed home with all of them when they were little. I worked part time later after they were in school. I'm very thankful to God for each of my children. I dedicate these chapters to them. My life would have been so empty and meaningless without them. I continue to pray for them, that God will protect and bless them.

Left: Christine pregnant for Andrea
Right: Colleen pregnant for Alan

Reflections

Written 6/01/2012

Yes, you called me to be a mother, a godly mother, and I feel as though I have failed my children, even though they are walking in your light and truth. I know each of us has a free will, but if I had reflected more of your light and love, then they would have craved you! Yet I know that you are the perfect parent yet a lot of your children walk away from you, thinking they know better how to run their lives.

Oh God redeem any of and all of my failures. Help me to trust you with all of my heart and lean not on my own understanding.

I prayed daily that God would comfort and strengthen them. Keeping them close to each other and to God. That they would keep their faith and grow to be Godly men and woman, husbands, wives, and fathers and mothers. I pray that God would protect them from evil influences, injuries, accidents and illness. That God would always help them know I loved them, even when I didn't get to talk to them or see them for long periods of time. Only God can protect our children, when they are beyond our reach!

A Mothers' Prayer

I wash the dirt from little feet, and as I wash, I pray,

"Lord, keep them ever pure and true to walk the narrow way."

I wash the dirt from little hands, and earnestly I ask,

"Lord, may they ever yielded be, to do the humblest task."

I wash the dirt from little knees, and pain, I pray,

"Lord may they be in the place where victories all won, and orders sought from thee,"

I scrub the clothes that soil so soon, and pray,

"Lord may his dress throughout eternal ages be thy robe of righteousness."

E'er many hours shall pass, I know, I'll wash these hands again; and there'll be dirt upon his pants before the day shall end.

But as he journeys on through life and learns of want and pain, Lord, keep his precious little heart cleansed from all sin and stain;

For soap and water cannot reach where Thou alone can see. His hands and feet, these I can wash – I trust his heart to Thee.

B. Ryberg, King's Business

******Christine's notes: Colleen wrote this on April 13, 1987, for a writing assignment. She lived in Groton, New York at the time. This story is about Colleen and I when we were children. All of the details are correct, except the names have been changed, and we were not Italian. Even though we often got each other the same presents, the amethyst rings in this story are not one of them.

The Interview

SUSAN CONNORS PUT HER BOOKS ON THE COUNTER AS SHE DROPPED into the nearest chair, "it's just not fair!"

"What's not fair?" Susan's mother asked, as she walked into the kitchen.

"Last weekend it rained and I didn't have anything to do. This weekend is going to be beautiful and I have tons of homework", Susan complained.

"A ton of homework?" Susan's mother asked.

"Well, it's just in English, but it will take all weekend to do it." Susan declared.

"What do you have to do?"

"I have to interview someone and then write a story about it," Susan said with despair in her voice. "I'll have a hard-enough time asking them the questions, let alone having to write down all the answers," Susan explained.

"You could pack your tape recorder in your book bag. Then when you begin your interview just ask the person if you can use it."

Susan brightened, "Wow mom, why didn't I think of that? Then all I have to do is ask the questions."

"Now you're thinking," said her mother.

"Yeah, but who can I interview?" Susan asked glumly.

"How about the Tommassi twins, you wanted to get to know them better."

Susan thought about it for a moment. She had never known identical twins before. They were new in the neighborhood. She had met them in school because they had the same homeroom. "They even talk to each other in another language!" protested Susan, "they're always together!"

"It's called Italian. Twins are usually very close. You can interview both of them and find out what it's like to be a twin."

"OK," Susan said as she jumped up. "I'll go upstairs and change." 20 minutes later Susan raced down the stairs. "Mom does what I have on look OK or does it clash?" Mrs. Connor looked at her 12-year-old daughter admiringly. Susan had a habit of choosing wild colors and putting them together but her soft pink top and bold purple shorts today were fine. Her cheeks were rosy and her blue eyes sparkled. The sunlight shone through her blonde hair, as it fell around her shoulders.

She would've looked adorable in a burlap bag, thought Mrs. Connors. She had a charming disposition in spite of her exaggerated complaints about her homework. "You look fine honey," she said smiling.

"Thanks mom", Susan said "I'll see you later." as she grabbed her loaded book bag and headed out the door.

Susan saw Anna and Mena Tommassi, as she walked up the sidewalk to their home. They were playing some sort of game out back. They were both dressed in pink but their outfits did not match, she noticed. Still they looked like the same person. Both had long dark hair pulled back into a ponytail with pink ribbons. They were both smaller than Susan, even though they were all the same age. Their olive-toned skin made it look like they had a tan all the time. "Hi" Susan said cheerfully walking closer to them.

"Oh hello, come in and join us Susan" one of them asked. Susan couldn't tell them apart.

"Well," Susan answered "I was wondering if you could help me?

I have to interview someone for a homework assignment. Could I interview the both of you?"

"Oh yes, that would be great. We've never been interviewed before" the other girl answered excitedly.

"Do you mind if I use my tape recorder?"

"Oh no, but let's go up to our bedroom so you can plug it in."

Susan studied the girls as they took the lead up to their room. She had to find a way to tell them apart. Their bedroom was twice the size of her own room, Susan thought, but of course there were two of them! White ruffles were everywhere, at the windows, on the canopy beds, around the white pillows and the soft pink chairs. The carpeting was the same color as the pink chairs and there were small, pink, rose buds on the wallpaper.

"What a beautiful room!" Susan exclaimed. "I thought twins always had twin beds," Susan said as she looked at the canopy beds again.

"No, not always. Ever since we were babies mama kept us together because we were more content. She says lots of times we would be right next to each other sucking each other's thumbs."

"Oh" Susan said smiling "that must've been so cute! My first question is, who is who, and how can I tell you apart?"

The girls looked at each other and grinned. "Anna has a small beauty mark on the right side of her face, but to make it easier I'll put my hair down, so you can tell us apart."

"Thank you, Mena, that's really helps," Susan said, feeling relieved.

"You can plug your recorder in here," Anna suggested.

Susan plugged in the tape recorder and turned it on. "Do you ever play tricks on anyone?"

"One time we did. I wanted to put some make up on her beauty mark to cover it up and I put some eyeliner on my face to make a dot like hers. Papa got us confused and punished Anna for something I did wrong. When I found out I felt so bad, we agreed never to do that again!"

"Do you like the same kinds of things?" asked Susan.

"I say half-and-half." Mena answered.

"We like the same clothes, colors, friends and food," Anna said "but we don't like the same instruments and subjects in school."

Mena interrupted. "I like piano, organ and any kind of keyboard instrument. Also, I like math and computers. But Anna likes guitar and violin, history, English etc."

"You don't always wear the same clothes, do you?" Susan inquired.

"Not always. Mostly just on special occasions. But a lot of times we end up wearing the same color. It's just a coincidence," Mena exclaimed. "we really don't plan it that way. Nonna and Nonno buy us a lot of clothes that match; but our parents mostly just buy us the same colors so everything can be interchanged. That way we have twice as many outfits."

"That's a good idea, but who's Nonna and Nonno? Susan asked.

"Oh, that's Italian for grandfather and grandmother" Anna replied.

"Do you ever get tired of celebrating your birthdays together?"

"Oh no" Anna said, and Mena shook her head too.

"It wouldn't seem like my birthday without Mena. For our last birthday, we gave each other the same present and we didn't know until after we had opened our presents. They were identical birthstone rings. We were both amazed because we really had no idea. See?" Anna held out her hand.

"Oh, that's a pretty ring," Susan exclaimed." Is it a real amethyst?"

"Yes, and we both saved our money for the whole year and we guarded our secret well," "Mena declared.

"Lots of times we get each other the same birthday card, but we have never done this before." Anna added.

"Which one of you is older?"

"I am" Mena said "by three minutes."

"What is your middle name?"

"Mine is Mena Amee and Anna's is Anna Marie."

Reflections

"Oh, I see you have the same initials in your name, but they're just reversed. Do you ever fight?"

"No, not really, sometimes we argue but not too much," Mena answered. "We hurt each other's feelings more than anything else. If Mena does or says anything selfish or thoughtless, I get hurt and I just cry or get quiet. I hardly ever get mad at her; it just hurts too much."

Anna added "yeah me too, only sometimes I get angry instead of crying," Anna said. "A lot of times we are feeling the same way, we just need to talk about it. I feel just awful when we're not getting along. It's like a part of myself hates me.

"We usually get things straightened out quickly," Mena added.

"You're best friends then?"

"Yes, we are, but we like to have lots of other friends too." Mena said.

"Do you talk to each other a lot in Italian, so others can't understand what you're saying?"

"We don't speak in Italian for that reason, it's just easier sometimes. We were almost 2 years old before we said anything in English or Italian. Mama says we had language all our own. Mena exclaimed.

"Wow" said Susan "you even sound a lot alike."

Mena and Anna giggled. "You're going to have an awfully hard time figuring out who said what on the tape recorder," Mena said. "We can't even tell ourselves apart on one of those."

"Oh dear, oh well, I'll just write the story about twins. I won't quote you." Susan said smiling. "That's all the questions I had."

"Do you like pizza?" Anna asked

"Yes, I love pizza."

"Why don't you stay for dinner. Papa always makes homemade pizza on Friday night," Mena requested.

"Oh, that's terrific."

"Let's go finish the game. We will teach you how to play it. It's called *tomborelli*. Maybe we can teach you some Italian words too." Anna suggested.

******Christine's notes: Here are a couple other of my favorite stories of
our growing up as identical twins that I'd like to add.*

Colleen and I were on the high honor roll and got similar grades in school. In junior high, one time, we both had math and English tests the next day. We decided we didn't want to study for both, so we figured we would save time and take each other's classes. I did the English classes; Colleen did the math classes. Everything was fine, until I forgot to tell Colleen that my math class was in a different room, down the hallway. She went to the class she thought was mine and realized it wasn't the right math class.

By that time, the bell rang and she was in the middle of the hallway not knowing where to go. Just then the principal walked down the hall and questioned her why she was there. She immediately started crying, as we never got in trouble. He took her to his office and sat her down, giving her a Kleenex and asked her what happened. When she was finally able to talk and told him the situation, he started laughing. He thought it was so funny. He looked up where she was supposed to be in my class, gave her a note and sent her on her way.

Another time Colleen was sick, and so I decided to try an experiment. I went to half of her classes and half of mine and they marked us both present that day.

A favorite story of mine, happened when our daughter Andrea and her now husband, Jeremy, were friends, and beginning to date. We were at our church in Marathon, New York for a special event going on. Colleen had come in from out of town that day, so I had not seen her yet.

I talked to Jeremy and I was wearing a black dress with pastel flowers on it. This was upstairs in the church. He went downstairs and saw Colleen coming in the church. He had never met her before, and didn't understand about identical twins. He saw her and she was wearing the exact same dress, only she was pregnant. He thought he was crazy and went to Andrea and said "Andrea, Andrea I don't know what's going on but I just saw your mom and she's pregnant?" Andrea immediately knew what was happening, she was laughing and said "Oh no that's my aunt Colleen!"

Even though for most of our adult life we lived out of state from each other, we often, without telling each other, would show up with the same dresses, coats, haircuts. It was uncanny. One time she came home and we had both bought the same medium, royal, blue trench coat. Unbelievable.

Another time Colleen was out of state for a week with her husband to a conference. Her middle son, John, was only a toddler. My mom, his grandmother who lived 10 minutes away was taking care of him. My mother called me a day after Colleen left and asked if I could come over. John was really upset and missing his mommy. When I got there, as I walked in with my little girl Andrea, I could hear him crying. As soon as I walked in the door he stopped and looked at me. You could see in his eyes like he was thinking, she's not quite like mom, but she's close enough. Needless to say, I held him and read him stories for a few hours and after that he was fine.

There was another funny time, when Colleen was living in Georgia, and her daughter Christina was about four years old. I had come down to surprise her for our birthday. I showed up at her door with balloons and a ribbon that said "surprise" on a banner. I knocked on the door, and Christina opened the door. I could see Colleen in the kitchen talking on the phone. Christina looked at me and then look back at her mom and then back to me, and said "Hi mommy?" I stayed with her in her room that week and she called me "mommy" all week.

Invitation to Christ

INVITING CHRIST TO COME INTO MY HEART AS A CHILD, WAS AS natural to me as breathing! My mother read to us from the Bible, along with Bible stories every night. She lived out her faith in front of us, calling on God in prayer whenever she had a need! She recalled the miracle surrounding my twin sister's and my birth.

We always went to church on Sundays. It was not Sunday unless it included church. If there was a blizzard or sickness, we would simply have church at home. I always remember being a Christian, surrendering my life to Christ, and giving him everything, including my future.

Putting Him first was more real when I was 13 years old at Word of Life Island summer camp. The island was for teens in Schroon Lake, New York in the Adirondack mountains. I was in chapel, and although I do not remember what the speaker was talking about, I do remember tearing out of the building as soon as the service ended.

I ran as far away from people as I could, as fast as I could, to the other side of the island. By the water, I sat on a big rock and sobbed, pouring my heart out to God and giving him my life! I knew I could not live my life without the power of God! I needed him to live and breathe! I was very shy and scared of life in general, I needed God to help me live for him. I was bolder after that, carrying my Bible to school, and being a quiet witness for God!

Trusting God

I'D LIKE TO SAY THAT I'VE ALWAYS TRUSTED GOD; FROM THE TIME in my childhood that I first received Christ into my heart. Then later as a teen, dedicating my whole life to him, but sadly I cannot. I have always endeavored to be a good Christian and wholly trust in God, but I've always struggled with fear.

Fear gripped my young life. Fear of people, fear of failure, fear of difficult circumstances, fear of evil, fear of life's hardships, and the general fear in the world, plagued me. Fear of failure and criticism were huge. I was a people pleaser. I certainly wanted to please my mom, and God of course. My favorite verse in high school was, "I sought the Lord and he delivered me from all my fear."

I got married right after high school and I remember as a young woman thinking, that if life presented terrible crushing difficulties, I might not be able to handle it. My own father took his life, and I wondered would I as well.? It haunted me. I was young, and I got married because I wanted someone to love, protect, and take care of me. I was fearful of going out into this world alone. I knew the verse that God wouldn't give us more than we could handle, but I failed to believe it fully and understand that.

What turned me around was Beth Moore's Bible study "Believe in God" and truly believing God's word. What He says, He will do. His promises are especially for me, He does not go back on His

Word. Praise God after fifty plus years of living, I'm free to trust God fully. The curse of fear over me is broken. I don't care anymore if people don't understand or approve. If I know God is pleased with me that's all I care about. It helps if Rich, my husband, and my sister, and my mom approve, but that's all.

Moments With My First Son

MY ELDEST SON ALAN, WHO IS NOW TWELVE YEARS OLD, WAS BORN on a Sunday. Very appropriate for a minister's son, I would say. That was the first Sunday my husband had ever taken off. He didn't have a choice, for Alan was born between Sunday School and Worship Service.

Three years later we were pastoring in Salisbury, Maryland. We were half an hour from the beautiful Atlantic Ocean, which more than compensated for my home sickness of missing the wonderful hills, lakes and waterfalls of Up-State New York. Alan was fascinated with a big shell I had. He would frequently hold it carefully.

One day He put it up to his ear and was awed! "Mommy, God is talking to me!" he whispered.

"He is?" I said, realizing the still small voice of God I had described to him, was, in his mind translated to the sound of the sea he heard in that shell. Alan was so excited and thrilled. His big brown eyes were full of wonder as he listened "to God" in the shell. He stood so very quiet to hear "every word."

I was very touched as I watched my young son, and prayed that as he grew, he would always stop and listen for the still small voice of God consistently telling him right from wrong. I prayed that he would be obedient to that voice to spare him all the heartache and trouble that disobedience would cause. I was very thankful he had learned the concept of Gods' voice so early in life.

Later that year we went for a visit back home. Alan's out-going personality, boldness and personal conviction, led him to lecture an unsaved, Italian Uncle about the woes and sin of smoking! He then proceeded to diligently pray for him for years. His uncle did quit smoking a few years ago, when his little girl developed an allergy to smoke!

Alan has always loved "all creatures great and small." He wants to be an animal trainer, or a veterinarian when he grows up. One fine summer day, when he was six, I heard an earth shattering "Mom!" It was an excited scream, not a tortured one, so I knew no one's arm had been cut off! But since none of my sons were screamers, I ran outside not knowing what to expect! Alan was on all fours examining the side walk! As I stepped closer, I could see he was enthralled with a big bug!

"Isn't it beautiful?" he said, almost reverently. I gulped, I had taught him to appreciate God's beautiful handiwork in nature but I was referring to rainbows, sunsets, oceans, waterfalls, and animals, not bugs!

"Beautiful" would surely be an exaggeration, I thought. I looked closer and strangely enough I could actually see a lot of beauty! It looked like an over grown fly with transparent wings. The top of its head and back looked like God had reached down and painted a stroke of translucent green. I had to admit it, was the most beautiful bug I had ever seen!

At age ten, my son amazed me again. Alan had been down the road to our neighbor's house, lifting weights with his friend, Doug, who was 12 years old, and his father (a regular event on Monday and Thursday evenings). When Alan came home, he burst in the house jumping up and down. He was obviously very excited about something. "Mom, you won't believe what just happened," he exclaimed. "Doug and Kenny just got saved. Isn't that the most, greatest thing that's ever happened?"

"Yes, it certainly is, tell me about it," I said in amazement.

Alan proceeded to tell me that after they finished weight lifting, he went up to Kenny's room to play (Kenny is 8 years old). All three of my sons had been telling Doug and Kenny about Jesus and that He needs to live in their hearts.

Alan said, "We were just playing and Kenny asked me, "How do you get Jesus in your heart? So, I told him all about it, that you have to pray and ask God to forgive you for your sins, and invite him in. So then, I asked him if he wanted to pray. He said "yes," and then we went into his closet.

"You went into the closet?" I asked, confused.

"Well, yes, you know Kenny has a big walk-in closet. He has a light in there and everything! It's his very special place to go. It's his very own private places...It's his secret hideout. He goes in there all the time to play or be by himself. He loves his closet!" Then, Alan went on, "I told him that he had to really mean it, or it wouldn't work!"

"Oh, I see," I said, hiding my amusement at the way he worded his explanation of sincerity.

"I prayed first, then Kenny prayed," Alan continued. "Kenny repeated after me. So, we prayed that Jesus would forgive him of everything he had ever done wrong as a kid, and to come into his heart. Then Doug knocked on the door and asked what we were doing. So I told him, and he said he wanted to pray too. So I prayed with him."

"In the closet?" I asked.

"Yeah, it was so great, Mom! When we got all done, I hugged them and told them that it was the most intelligent thing they had ever done!"

"That's marvelous," I said. The tears were streaming down my face as I hugged him. "I'm so proud of you, Alan. What did their parents say? Do they know?" I inquired.

"Yeah, I went right out and told them that their sons had prayed and Jesus was living in their hearts and that they were real Christians now!"

"What did they say?" I asked.

"They didn't say anything, they just looked at each other. Mom, I've got to call Dad!" And then Alan raced to the phone.

That will be a night none of us will ever forget. Alan's enthusiasm and excitement spread over our household, like sunlight permeates a room. Later in the week I called the boys' mother and invited them to church. She told me her husband was Catholic, but didn't care for the church nearby. So the only time they went to church was on Christmas or Easter. But she thought it would be a good idea for her sons to come to our church, because she knew they needed to know more about God. She said that she would ask her husband if they could come. Well, the boys have been coming to church ever since. At Christmas last year, their parents and grandmother came to see them in our Christmas program.

My husband quizzed Alan afterward about exactly what he had told the boys the night of their conversion. Sure enough, he had covered all the bases of the plan of salvation, and had quoted enough scripture to make it authentic. The following Sunday the boys came to Sunday School and church. Before church, my husband talked to them. They knew exactly what they had done and why, and they didn't mind at all if the whole church knew. Needless to say, our worship was enhanced as we praised God for two young boys and A CLOSET OF PRAYER!

The boys have not missed a Sunday. They knew nothing about Noah or the story of creation, or any of the basic Bible stories. I was delighted one Sunday when our lesson was about prayer and the scripture "But thou, when thou prayest, enter into thy closet, and when thou hast shut thy door, pray to thy Father which is in secret; and thy Father: which seeth in secret, shall reward thee openly." Matthew 6:6. I asked Kenny to read the verse, and as he did, he lit up like a Christmas tree. As soon as he finished reading, he looked up to me so excited and said..."I did that! I did that!" I smiled and said, "Yes, Kenny, you certainly did." I was so pleased that he grasped the significance of his closet prayer and what Jesus had said.

Kenny and his brother Doug have attended Sunday School and

church for two years now. Alan has been a big influence on the whole family. Just recently because of Alan's faithfulness and prayer his father led these two boys' parents to Christ in our living room. "And Jesus said unto them, "If ye have faith as grain of mustard seed" Matthew 17:20. "A child shall lead them" Isaiah 11:6

*******Christine's notes: *The following story Colleen wrote February 10, 1987. It was an assignment for a writing course she took, while she was living at Groton, New York.*

Alan's Disappointment

ALAN AWOKE TO THE SWEET SOUND OF BIRDS CHIRPING OUTSIDE the window. A gentle breeze blew the white ruffled curtains. He sat up and gazed out at the beautiful blue sky behind the big red barn. He was going to spend the whole month at his grandparents farm! It was so great to be here, he thought to himself. Away from the city, his brothers and everything!

Just then a brooding thought came to his mind, away from school, a terrible sadness crept over him. He felt an ache inside that threatened to crush him and dispel any joy and happiness he felt. "Oh why did I have to fail third grade?" Alan lamented. He got up quickly and shook his head with determination. "I'm not gonna let anything ruin this day or any others for a whole month!" He said out loud as he dressed and dashed out the door.

He ran downstairs. "Good morning Alan" Grandma said she hugged him. "I love you"

"I love you too," said Alan. Grandma kept on hugging him like she was trying to make up for all the hugs she missed since he saw her last. Grandma had such a way of making you feel loved. Just like you were her most favorite person in the whole world!

Alan felt happy and then sad, all at the same time. Some big tears started to roll down his cheeks. "Grandma, I feel so dumb. I tried so hard and I still didn't pass." He buried his face in her dress and wept. He knew that Grandma felt his pain. Without looking, he knew she had tears in her eyes too.

She led him over to a big chair in the living room and gently sat him down beside her. Alan rested his head on his shoulder and she patted his hand. They must have sat there only a few minutes, but it seemed like a gloriously long time. Then Grandma said "Alan somethings take people more time to learn than others. I remember when I was your age."

"You do?" Alan exclaimed.

"Yes," Grandma smiled and continued. "I couldn't sew a stitch. My my sisters all sewed, but it just didn't interest me."

"You sew now." Alan interrupted.

"Yes, I had an aunt who took me aside and showed me some shortcuts and really made sewing fun! I have never been a great seamstress like my sisters, and it still is not my most favorite thing to do, but I can make a terrific pie!"

"You sure can!" Alan said assuredly.

"Alan, we all have different abilities and all so some things, are harder for us. But if we make the most of out of what the good Lord has given us, then he is pleased and we have nothing to be ashamed of. As long as we don't give up! You are very special, sensitive and good boy."

Alan was feeling a lot better when Andrea, Alan's cousin pounded up the steps and came in the front door. "Hi Alan, Hi Grandma," she exclaimed. They were the same age, and she was a lot of fun! She had long blonde hair and smiling blue eyes. She lived down the road from their grandparents.

Grandma smiled and patted Alan's shoulder, "Why don't you two go get your grandfather and tell him breakfast is ready?"

"Race ya!" Alan called and she bolted out the door. Alan quickly caught up with her and passed her. By then, Lady and Spirit, the farm dog and cat joined in the race to the barn. The chickens scattered to make way for them.

"Grandpa" they yelled. Grandpa stepped out of the barn into the sunlight as they reached the barn.

"I won" Alan said, smiling, all out of breath.

Reflections

"Breakfast is ready, Grandpa" said Andrea.

"Well I was beginning to wonder if we were going to eat this morning" Grandpa teased. Alan and Andrea hugged their grandfather and skipped and laughed all the way back to the house. After breakfast, Alan suggested "Let's go down by the creek, maybe I can find some salamanders or frogs."

"OK." Andrea replied.

"Are we still best friends?" Alan asked.

"Yes!" said Andrea.

"I failed the third grade" Alan said bluntly.

"You did?"

"Yes," Alan answered "do you like me just the same?"

"Sure I do!"

Alan said earnestly, "You're my best friend. Remember how you helped me learn to ride my bike? Or the time you cheered me up when I had stitches in my hand? You've taught me a lot about baseball, and soccer".

A few minutes passed, then Andrea said excitedly "I've got a great idea! Maybe after supper, mom would let me come back down to Grandma's and we could play school! It would be fun and I'll help you all I can."

Alan thought it over, maybe with Andrea's help he could learn to like school! "OK, we'll give it a try" said Alan.

Instructor

Alan, my oldest son, taught his younger brothers to play lacrosse, a Native American game that has grown in popularity over the last several decades. The three of them played for their high school in Tully, New York. On the team, they won everything that year! They got a huge trophy.

Alan went into the Marines after high school, John and Dan continued to play. Scouts came to see their games, and John ended up going to Virginia Military Academy and received a partial lacrosse scholarship. Dan had a number of offers: Duke, AFA, Princeton, Yale, West Point, and Navy Academy. He ended up going to the Naval Academy on a full scholarship! 250k! Amazing!

I remember when my sons were in middle school, and realizing we would never be able to afford to help them go to college. I started praying that God would give them opportunities and totally provide for them to do so. God used Alan and lacrosse to answer that prayer!

After the Marines, Alan tried going back to school (forestry). He had just gotten back from the Iraq war in 2004, but was having a hard time of it. Being confined to a classroom again was not only restrictive and monotonous but impossible for him. He had had a hard enough time getting through high school.

He was very smart, but sitting in a classroom drove him crazy. Then some of the material seemed redundant, and the other students ridiculous and immature. After the realities of war nothing seems to matter! So, he was not able to continue. But God used him to help his younger brothers! Now he teaches private lacrosse lessons to anyone who wants to learn.

Motherhood and the Law

Up until I became a mother, I was a perfectly upstanding, law abiding citizen. Actually, it wasn't until after my second child, John, was born, that I had my first run in with the law. They say motherhood changes you; but I didn't realize, that would involve temporary insanity or absence of mind. Or that I would break the law and not even know it; in three different states mind you!

The first time I had ever been stopped by a police officer, it was night time. I was living in Salisbury, Maryland in 1980. I was very upset because my five-month-old baby, John, was very sick for the first time. I had taken him to the doctor and home again. His aunt Lorraine was there to watch him, while I went to get the medicine he needed.

I came to a red light, looked both ways and proceeded through the red light. A police officer stopped me and I had no idea what I had done wrong. It was the first time in my 26 years that I had even spoken to a police officer. I burst into tears and sobbed as he said "Lady do you know that you went through a red light back there?"

I cried, "No I didn't, I'm sorry, my baby is sick and he needs his medicine!" Was all I could get out. The officer was very kind and gave me his handkerchief. Unbeknownst to me, he knew who I was, the minister's wife, where his wife's family went to church. He gave me a warning and sent me on my way. The warning is still in my sons' baby book. I often wondered if he thought at first, my crying was an act to get out of a ticket, but very shortly, I knew he didn't feel that way at all. I didn't know until later that he knew who I was. That was a traumatic experience for me.

The second infraction was in Ohio. We lived in the parsonage beside the church. It was literally like living inside a fishbowl, with houses all around us. Having grown up in the country, I missed the open spaces in the countryside terribly.

One day, when I had our one and only car, I packed up the boys, put some food in a basket, and we headed for the country. I just drove out of town, being careful to remember the direction, so I could get back. I remember I found a meadow, and behind some trees, there was a dirt road. I pulled in and just parked. We all scrambled out and headed across the meadow and through the trees to the next meadow. We enjoyed a lovely, leisurely picnic; the boys played and we had a wonderful afternoon. Then we picked up and headed back to the car.

We were halfway across the meadow, when I looked up and saw a police car barreling toward us. The policeman jumped out and said "Is that your green Chevy car parked over there?"

"Yes" was all I could say.

"What are you doing?"

"We were having a picnic" I replied.

I was surprised by his response, "Well lady can't you go to a park?"

"I'm fairly new in town and I didn't know where any of the parks were", I said. "I didn't see any signs, I'm really sorry, I didn't know it was posted." (so much for being in a free country), I thought.

He proceeded to say that the farmer was having trouble with kids using his property to do drugs etc., so when he saw the car, he just assumed it was the kids. Anyway, that was it. He got in his patrol car and drove away across the field. My little boys and I walked across the field and went back home. They were all very quiet going home. We had quite an adventurous picnic!

My third encounter with police was in upstate New York. It was a Saturday morning in the summertime and my sons and I were driving my two nieces back home to Harford, from our home in Otisco. It was a cool day, so we had the windows up and playing music on the radio. We were all singing and having a wonderful time. All the sudden I happened to look in my rearview mirror. There were lights flashing from a police car that was right on my tail. Then I heard the siren. I was so shocked, it scared me to death and I slammed on the brakes without pulling over. The officer was yelling as I rolled down the window. "Didn't you hear the siren?"

I replied "No sir, we had the windows rolled up and the radio was on and we were singing. What did I do, you scared me to death?"

He stopped and just stared at me as if all of a sudden realizing he didn't have a fugitive running from the law, just a mom, distracted and clueless about exceeding the speed limit on this country road. He just took a deep breath and looked into the car, where all five children were speechless, mouth open, and staring wide-eyed at the officer. They had never seen a police officer up close and personal like this.

Finally, he said "Lady you have five children in the car, you need to slow down!" With that he turned and went back to his car and drove away. No warning or anything! I was dumbfounded. And of course, I drove within the speed limit the rest of the way, slower and much more carefully.

When I started the car and my youngest son Daniel, said "Mommy I'm scared."

I said "Honey you don't have to be afraid it's all over now."

"He had a gun!" was all he said next.

"Yes dear that's in case he finds a bad guy but he knew we weren't bad. He just wanted to protect us."

My brushes with the law scared me straight. No more lawbreaking for me. Confronted three times for three different reasons, no repeat offender here. To be honest, I still love picnics, going to meadow, driving with music loud, and since my boys are grown and moved away, I tend to occasionally go faster than the speed limit.

The Red Cross

I ONLY WORKED AT THE RED CROSS FOR THREE YEARS. BUT DURING that time my life would change dramatically and would never be the same again. I had been working in Syracuse, New York for an ear, nose and throat physicians' office for a few months. However, I did not like that job at all. It did not suit me. So, I called the Red Cross, and sent in my resume. I quit my job before Christmas and started training with the Red Cross in January 1989.

I was so much happier! A nurse, who, just happened to live right down the road from me, trained me. Although I hate needles myself, and had never donated blood; I became skilled at phlebotomy (Finding a good vein for blood donation). I was a per-diem nurse. I would fill in for the staff at different locations around the Syracuse region, where they were having blood drives.

I didn't think I would like the travel, but I grew to love it. The freedom it would allow me was intoxicating. I traveled eight counties, and could pick my own schedule. I really enjoyed traveling the picturesque countryside of upstate New York! I didn't have a cell phone, but I never got lost and whenever I had a problem with my car, God always sent someone to help me.

I made several good friends with the staff and they were always glad to see me. I was the extra help when they were short staffed! We were really very much like a MASH unit, going into churches, fire halls, VFW lodges, schools, etc. We would go in and set up shop, working all day as a cohesive team, then tearing down. It was great fun, especially when I got to work with all my friends.

I remember when the First Gulf War started. People came in droves to donate blood for the troops. We told people to hold off, because if they donated now, they couldn't donate again for 56 days. There were no ground troops deployed yet. We didn't know the future.

I only ever worked part time, 3 to 4 days a week. I also got paid for all my travel time on the road, so it was good for me. I did travel in all kinds of weather and sometimes traveled two hours, one way, to go to work. Cooperstown and Oneonta, New York, and Sayre, Pennsylvania were the furthest I had to go. We also used to go to factories, for example, Ithaca gun. I actually didn't like those places so much. My favorite places were the little country churches, in small communities. The little ladies of the church would always fix us a good lunch and treated us like royalty! We had a small crew and it was just right.

Colleen's Graduation from Nursing School

Reflections

Songs and Sayings I Like

"You are like a waterfall running wild and free, but still I hear your still small voice when you speak to me."
None But You
"Oh my delight is in you Lord, all my hopes, all my strength, all my dreams, I live to bring Him praise, you are the reason I live."
Show me - Revelation Third Day
Before the Morning - Josh Wilson "dare to believe, the pain you've been feeling can't compare to the joy that's coming, Wait, press on, hurt before healing, darkest before the morning..."
He Reigns - Chris Tomlin "I will rise, God will do what he said."
"Manners are a sensitive awareness of the feelings of others." Emily Post
"The task ahead is never as great as the power behind us (the power of God)."
On Worship: He always wanted people to be totally committed. God wants to restore us to his original idea.
God doesn't need us, but he wants our attention and affection. James 4:8
Thoughts on Psalms 23, written 8/7/18:
"You Lord, are the one I looked to. You have everything I need. You give me rest and quiet, good places; where I am safe and protected. You refresh me, beside quiet waters and you restore my soul. Because of your Holy name, you lead me along the right path for my life. Even this path of losing Rich, and my life has been so hard; you have been right here with me. I have no reason to fear because you've got ahold of me; Your rod of protection and staff of comfort will keep me secure. You prepare great things for me, even when there are naysayers all around, you call me out and proclaim I am yours and that I am special. I am overwhelmed at the goodness and mercy you show me. I will dwell with you forever!"
"The Lord is exalted above all the earth."

"Do not be afraid or discouraged because of this vast army. For the battle is not yours, but God's." 2 Chronicles 20:25

"So do not fear. For I am with you. Do not be dismayed for I am your God. I will strengthen you and help you. I will uphold you with my righteous right hand. For I am the Lord your God who takes hold of your right hand and says to you, do not fear; I will help you." Isaiah 41:10 -13

"Vindicate me, oh God plead my cause......rescue me from the deceitful and wicked men...you are God my strong hold...put your hope in God." Psalm 43

"For you, oh God, tested us...You refined us like silver...We went through fire and water, but you brought us to a place of abundance." Psalm 66:10,12

"I will restore to you the years that the locusts have eaten, says the Lord." Joel 2:25

*******Christine's notes: I sang the following song with my daughter Rebekah, and it is recorded on our family album "Go the Distance." I didn't realize this meant as much to Colleen as it did to me, until I saw it written out in her journals. I know she felt this way many times in her life:*

He'll Find A Way by Donna Douglas

At times is the load is heavy, at times the road is long,
When circumstances come your way and you think you can't go on,
when you're feeling at your weakest, Jesus will be strong.
He'll provide an answer, when you found all hope is gone,
He'll find a way.

Chorus

For I know that if He can paint a sunset, and put the stars in place,

Reflections

I know if He can raise up the mountains and calm the storm-tossed
waves,
and if He can conquer death forever and open heavens gates,
Then I know for you, He'll see you through,
He'll find a way.

At times your heart is breaking with the pain that's so intense,
All you hold are broken pieces to a life that makes no sense,
He wants to lift you up and hold you and mend each torn event.
He'll pick up the pieces that you saw had all been spent,
He'll find a way.

Chorus

For I know that if He can paint a sunset, and put the stars in place,
I know if He can raise the mountains and calm the storm-tossed
waves,
And if He can conquer death forever and open heavens gates, then
I know for you, He'll see you through, he'll find a way.

Colleen Loran & Christine Heath

******Christine's notes: The following was written when Colleen was in Ohio and it was published in the local Newspaper, Kentucky Ave., Mansfield, OH.*

Christmas at Grandpa's house

At Christmas time we would travel to my Grandparent's home in upstate New York. It was always snowing when my parents, two sisters, and my brother and I began the trip. Our anticipation would grow every mile, so that when we came to the town nearest my grandfather's home, we would announce to the world that it was Grandpa's town, and Grandpa's bridge, etc. As we turned down the country lane, we would sit on the edge of our seats, straining to see which of us would see Grandpa's house first.

It was so picturesque, a modest white house, with trees and snow falling on the beautiful countryside. Grandpa always had wreaths in each window, surrounding an electric candle. Our excitement was explosive by the time we climbed out of the car into Grandpa's arms. He always greeted us at the door with lots of kisses and warm hugs. I suppose to slow down the stampede! His Christmas tree was the most beautiful I've ever seen, year after year.

Love was so thick, it just hung around us, warming our hearts and then our hands and feet. I don't remember the gifts I received. Whatever Grandpa gave me was wonderful because it was from him. He was not a wealthy man in this world's eyes; his wealth was a different kind. Wisdom, love and values were bestowed upon us in great abundance. I will always remember my Grandfather's gentle, quiet way. He read the Bible at breakfast, and his prayers, though hardly audible, were powerful. For you see, he didn't just pray and read the Bible at Christmas, he lived that way all year round!

Reflections

Christmas Eve

I celebrated Christmas with my sons and sisters in 1991 on Christmas Eve. We went to an early Christmas Eve Service together at Homer Baptist Church. It was down the street from where I lived, in a big, old, beautiful, Victorian house, upstairs apartment. We had a wonderful time and afterwards we went to my place and sang, opened presents and laughed. I loved that memory. Years later, when we were in Georgia, I would decorate the house, bake Christmas cookies and prepare for Christmas dinner ahead of time. Christmas Eve, three of us would head to church for Christmas Eve service and then we'd go home and have our own Christmas nativity story. Acting it out by Christina and her dad, in his bathrobe and her father's wooden cane. Precious, our cat, was usually baby Jesus, until a doll replaced her. She got too big for the cradle, and would simply not cooperate.

Christmas 2008

I looked out the window of the hospital in Rich's ICU room. It was a beautiful Florida sky; the sun was setting. Rich closed his eyes and finally was able to rest. God's peace came into the room. It was as if God in his mercy and love was hugging the three of us and telling us, "I'm here, I love you, it's all going to turn out fine. It's going to be all right, you'll see."

Christmas Day - Friday 2015

I was up about 4:30 am. I cleaned up the kitchen, got together some things I had to take later in the day, then I sat down to do my Christmas greeting on Facebook. About 7am I went back to bed, and no sooner got sleepy and was drifting back to sleep when our cat, Precious started rustling papers! That was our cue to get up and feed her! I'm usually up and had already fed her by now. I was debating whether to get up again, or not. I didn't want to reward her for disturbing me, but I also didn't want her to bother Rich. So, I finally got up and I was so glad I did! I always look to the skies and the sunrise, so I went out on my deck. I saw it, a beautiful rainbow! God was saying "Good morning and Merry Christmas" to me! I've never seen one like it before! What a gift! Thank you, Father! Thank you Precious! For getting me up, I would have missed it!

Christmas

If we lived closer, I would have had a Christmas tea and invited my family to my home. Since we don't, relax and have a cup of tea and some Christmas cookies or a scone. I would have served you. Hope you are having a blessed and happy Christmas day.

The 12 days of Christmas is really a song with rich symbolism of our Christian faith. Having to do with the 12 days after Christmas December 25 through January 5. It precedes the season of Epiphany, which involves a rich history of gift giving. I like this because Christmas is about Christ's birth. So, we should emphasize giving gifts to Him. Then, the 12 days after Christmas, give gifts to each other. This makes more sense to me and certainly extends the season which I love. So, my gifts aren't late after all!

There were many years that I dreaded the holidays, especially Christmas! It would start in the fall with Thanksgiving, and by Christmas it was really hard. I didn't want to feel bad and depressed and upset, but it was like a pot of water on low on a back burner and by Christmas, at one point or another it was boiling over. I would be terribly upset and crying. I tried to put it off by not thinking about it, putting on a good front for Christina and Rich. I would decorate the house, plan on holiday dinners, invite people over to celebrate with us, but after all that was over and I still hadn't heard from my sons I would cry.

Thankfully that's mostly over now. My sons have all grown, and except for one, have families of their own. I hear from them a lot more now. Still not as often as I would like but when we do talk or I see them, it is good.

Christmas is actually my favorite holiday, now & then.

Waiting on God

April 14, 2016

Just as a gardener plants, fertilizes, weeds and watches with expectancy to see the plants she has sown, to grow; we must do all we can, then wait with joy and anticipation to see the results--answers to our prayers. Preparing to wait!

We can wait in a doctor's office two ways; we can pace, ringing our hands, complaining loudly, fidget and get mad, or we can calmly read a good book we brought along just in case we would have to wait, crochet, knit or look through magazines, leisurely, because we never have time to do that! We can pray, read our Bible, if we have a smart phone do all the things on it, talk pleasantly and in an encouraging way to other ones while we're waiting.

What a difference it makes within us, and all the people around us, by how we choose to spend our time waiting. How do you wait on God for answers? We do all we can do, certainly, whatever God lays on our hearts. But then we must simply give it to Him and wait.

While waiting we can get our minds off the situation by praising God for the answers ahead of time, showing God our faith. Read good books, pursue hobbies and interests, visit and encourage friends and relatives, work on projects, get to know others by serving. Your life will be richer and time go by faster if you will seek to wait patiently, constructively, creatively, positively and productively. Lord keep me on the right path, while I wait for you. Psalm 69:13. Psalm 37:5, Psalms 4:1

Joy Comes in the Morning

I awoke early to the quiet sounds of birds sweetly singing outside my bedroom window. It was the day before Mother's Day. I was thanking God for all of His blessings, when my five-year-old daughter came running into the room. "Mommy, come into the kitchen, I have a surprise for you!" Her shoulder length blond hair was fluffed from sleeping, and her blue eyes sparkled as she spoke. Then she scampered away in her night shirt into the kitchen. I followed, wondering what she was up to. "See," she said, pointing to the counter, "I put all the silverware away for you, and you didn't even have to ask me to." She was so pleased with herself. "Happy Mother's Day," she said, hugging me. It was such an adorable gesture. My eyes misted and my heart was warmed by her thoughtfulness.

All day long my little ray of sunshine was busy making me surprises: a drawing, a flower from the yard, a homemade card. She even wrapped up her marbles to give to me! "Thank you, Lord, for my little girl," I whispered as we got ready to go to a mother/daughter luncheon at a nearby church. Then I reflected back to the painful circumstances in my life surrounding the time when I first realized I was pregnant with her. God had certainly turned my life around since then. It seemed like a lifetime ago now. I remembered how panicked, scared, confused and condemned I felt. Under normal circumstances I would have been ecstatic.

I had always wanted a fourth child. I had dreamed of a girl, after having had three adorable sons. They were now 13, 11 ½ and 10 years of age. But these were not normal circumstances! My life had fallen apart. I remembered pleading with God, "Please don't let me be pregnant now! I promise I won't see him again until the divorce is final." My mind screamed, "No, this can't be, not now!" Everything within me wanted to reject the thought that I was pregnant, but as the days wore on, I knew in my heart that I was.

How could I have let this happen? I had always done the right thing, serving God from a young age. I had been through so much.

Reflections

I knew I hadn't been as close to God recently, but I still did love Him. The disillusionment from my recent broken marriage had left me emotionally and spiritually devastated.

My former husband, who had been my confidant, friend, father of my three sons, pastor and spiritual leader, had been physically abusing me for the last five years of our eighteen-year marriage. At first, I blamed it on a head injury he sustained in a motorcycle accident in which he barely survived. After one week in ICU, and another week on the head trauma floor, he came home. How thankful we all were.

The first night home he started choking me in bed. He was very irrational and compulsive, and I was shocked and terrified! I didn't know this man who looked like my husband, but was acting like a stranger. Although I was confused and panicked, I was committed through sickness and health. I would stand by him and protect his reputation by telling no one about his abusive behavior. I felt certain that his injury and the medication he was on were the reasons. I gave his neurologist a whole list of adverse reactions I felt he was having due to all his medication. "Aggressive behavior" was one of them.

The doctor cut his medication in half, and told me that his brain scan had come back normal and there was nothing more he could do for him. He then suggested that he see a psychiatrist. I prayed that God would heal him and our marriage. We had been a close family and had a good marriage I thought, but now the periods of abuse were ravaging my love and taking its toll on all of us.

I was emotionally, mentally, and physically spent. I finally realized, after he repeatedly refused to get Christian counseling, that he didn't want help! Instead he denied everything. "Shrinks" were only for troubled souls in his congregation, certainly not for him. I knew that if he didn't admit his problem, get outside help and become accountable to someone, our marriage was lost.

Our home was an emotional roller coaster, and our sons were suffering the fallout. They were afraid of his rages and would scatter when he started to get angry. They were doing poorly in school, and

I knew they would possibly repeat the behavior they saw if this cycle of abuse was not broken. He had broken so many promises to me that I couldn't believe anything he said! I didn't trust him anymore. I was afraid for my sanity and my life, as he would one moment treat me like queen, and the next moment a servant.

So, after careful, agonizing thought and planning, I took my sons and left him! I knew it would be hard for them so I waited until they were out of school for the summer. But before that next fall their father had convinced them to come back and live with him. He blamed me and denied everything. I knew he was making it worse for them, making them choose sides. Then my sons "decided" they didn't even want to come and visit me on weekends! I was lost without them and missed them terribly. We had been so close. I was only ½ hour away, yet they were becoming very distant.

I gave up then. I didn't care anymore about being good or doing the right thing. Where had it gotten me? The pain in my heart was so severe it physically ached. I wanted to do anything to relieve that pain.

I had met Rich at my job. That first summer we just talked on the phone. He was cautious and concerned. We started seeing each other that fall. He was so nice, calm, and comfortable to be around, humble, with no ego to contend with. I felt safe and at ease for the first time in years. No more walking on egg shells waiting for the next angry explosion, demeaning words, or rough treatment. Rich was very kind to me and our relationship grew very quickly.

I knew we had been wrong even to be seeing each other before the divorce was final. This pregnancy complicated everything and ruined my Christian reputation. What would my sons think? I had not breathed a word of my suspicions to anyone. I was desperate and panicked. I had always been very pro-life, but now I was tempted to consider abortion. That way no one would have to know, I rationalized, not even Rich. Then everything would be okay, the divorce would be final and my life could go on. I was tormented with these thoughts, when the phone rang.

Reflections

It was my sister. She wanted to know how I was. I broke down sobbing and blurted out that I was pregnant. Since I hadn't been tested, she convinced me to come over the next day and she would pick up a test and be with me. When she hung up, I was relieved someone knew and was going to help me.

The next evening as I lay on her bed praying and pleading with God again, she came in and hugged me. "You are going to have a baby," she said, so caring and lovingly. I cried, then prayed, "Lord, make this child a blessing in spite of these circumstances."

The next day I told Rich. He was stunned and silent...then he hugged me and, to my surprise, prayed right then and asked God to forgive us and help us through what lay ahead.

After a few months my divorce was official, and we were married. We had a lovely, small wedding with beautiful flowers and music. Our family and friends were there and the pictures came out great!

It was a bright, cold morning in early November when our child was born. My loving, heavenly Father had seen my broken heart and gave me, not what I deserved, but the desire of my heart...a beautiful, healthy daughter, and a genuine, wonderful Christian husband. My sons would grow to love their little sister, Christina Joy. Our little girl is a testimony of God's goodness and mercy, assuring me of His forgiveness and care each time I look at her.

God had given me this verse before her birth and we used it at her dedication ceremony, along with Sandi Patti's song, *Masterpiece*. "For His anger endureth but a moment. In His favor is Life. Weeping may endure for a night, but joy cometh in the morning." Psalm 30:5 How true.

Colleen Loran & Christine Heath

Christina with Colleen

Masterpiece

"You made my whole being, you formed me in my mother's womb. You saw my bones being formed: as I took shape in my mother's body. When I was put together there, you saw my body as it was formed. I praise you because you made me in an amazing and wonderful way." Before you had a name or opened up your eyes, or anyone would recognize your face you were being formed so delicate in size, secluded in God's safe and hidden place. With your little tiny hands and little tiny feet and little eyes that shimmer like a pearl He breathed in you a song and to make it all complete He brought the masterpiece into the world. You are a Masterpiece, a new creation He has formed, and you're as soft and fresh as a snowy winter morn, and I'm so glad that God has given you to me little lamb of God, you are a Masterpiece.

"All the days planned for me were written in your book before I was even one day old. What you have done is wonderful; I know this very well."

Reflections

You called yesterday. I could hear the pain and despair in your voice. You asked me if I ever think of you.

If you only knew – if you could only grasp the many times during the day and night that I call out to God for you! I have to leave you on the altar of surrender. I pray God will touch you and reach your heart whatever it takes, to get thru to your heart how much I love you, and even more, how much God loves you! Yet you keep pushing Him away, and you can't believe or can't realize how much you are loved, and receive it.

You are stuck in your pain and your anger, and unforgiveness keeps you from moving ahead in your life. I pray soon, you will receive Revelation from God that He does love you, and that your mother deeply loves you!

You need deliverance from your past, your pain. God is ultimately the only one who can help you. Only when you allow God to help you, will you be able to stop pushing your family away from you! All of your family on both sides love you, but we don't know how to help you. Run to God for your salvation, for freedom from sin and bondage, and pain.

An Unforgettable Day in the Life of a Military Mom

AFTER HIGH SCHOOL, MY ELDEST SON, ALAN ENLISTED IN THE
Marines. He spent eight years altogether and traveled all over the
world, including Iraq. His experience in Iraq would take me on a
spiritual journey that I will never forget.

Alan had guarded embassies in New Delhi, India and Switzerland
during his first four years. Then he came home to marry Christie,
his beautiful high school sweetheart. The wedding took place just
months before 9/11.

After that attack on our country Alan reenlisted. He and Christie
were stationed at Camp Pendleton, CA. He was in the first Marine
Division when the war broke out. He saw his Comrades go over, but
his tour of duty was delayed. He called me after Christmas, 2003 to
inform me that he would be leaving for Iraq in early February, 2004.
He would be the lead scout and sharpshooter on his reconnaissance
team. He was in Baghdad and we prayed night and day for his safety.
We mobilized family, friends and church members to pray, sent cards
and boxes of anything to help my son and his comrades know that
we were with them in spirit, and to show our love and support.

It was in April, 2004 on Palm Sunday morning. I was at church.
It was about 10 AM and in between our two church services when,
all of a sudden, I felt a tidal wave sweep over me and I knew my son
was in extreme danger. I ran to the prayer room in our church. There

is a huge map of the world on one wall and I put my hand on Iraq as sobbed and cried out to God to protect my son, to surround him with holy angels. I felt as if I was right there with him, comforting and strengthening him with my prayers. I felt so close and connected to him at that time.

I've never had, before or since, such an intense impression to pray. Through the years and there had been many times when God would wake me up in the night to pray for my sons, especially Alan. And many times, during the middle of the day, I would feel to stop, and pray for him, especially when I would hear news of the war. But this was an overpowering, off the scale certainty that my son's life was hanging in the balance.

I prayed in the prayer room for a long time, then I had to join the choir for the second service. Of course, my mind was thousands of miles away, and I would whisper prayers, in between the songs. Then we sang "I Surrender All," and I knew that God was asking me if I would surrender my son to him that day. I had dedicated him to the Lord when he was a baby, and many times during the course of his life. But now, when he was facing the greatest battle of his life, could I surrender him?

I thought about Abraham determining to sacrifice his son, not knowing the outcome. I knew if Alan died, he would go to heaven. God had given me a verse in Zephaniah 3:20 about bringing him home. Was God telling me that He was going to take him home to heaven? Isn't that what all Christian mothers ultimately want for their children, to be safe with God in heaven? Was God telling me that day that He was going to take him early, in the prime of his life? I didn't know. I had to face the fact that, no matter what, I had to surrender my son to God again. After all, God had sacrificed His Son for me.

I did, right in the middle of church service while standing in the choir. I gave my son to God again. No one knew such a battle was going on within me. All during the service I wondered what was going on in Iraq. I kept praying, and had close friends and family praying also. Then, about 3:30 in the afternoon, as quickly as it came the urgency to pray completely left me, and I felt tremendous peace.

Later, on the National News, they said that riots had broken out on the streets of Baghdad. Right after that was when the thousand-man siege took place around Fallujah. I "knew" my son was involved in that. The news media had stated that, that week, Palm Sunday to Easter, 2004 was the worst fighting and highest casualties since the war started.

*******Christine's notes: That same day, on Palm Sunday, unaware of these events, I was in New York at church; Colleen was in Georgia. I was in choir too, and all of a sudden, I felt the urgency and felt a heavy burden to pray for Alan. I didn't know what was going on either but I got through with choir and prayed. Then on the way home I said to my husband and kids, "I just have this horrible feeling. You guys, as soon as I get home, I'm not going to eat with you, I'm going to just go in the bedroom and pray." I cried and cried for my sister, my nephew Alan, and just prayed that God would keep him safe that day. Then around 3 o'clock the burden lifted and I felt so much peace; that God was somehow answering my prayer. None of us knew what was going on that day. But God did, and over the years, Colleen and I, even though we've been far apart, have felt the same things. So here was another call to prayer together. Then two weeks later, when Alan called Colleen, we understood the urgency.*

No one in the family heard from Alan for weeks, not even his wife. Then one afternoon, out of the blue, Alan called me. He was safe! It was so good to hear his voice. He was traveling somewhere in Iraq. He couldn't tell me anymore than that. He said he was on a military satellite phone, and it sounded like he was in the same room. He said his ears had been hurt from explosions, and his feet were a mess from wearing his boots day and night, but he was fine. He didn't want to talk about the war.

We talked for an hour or more, and finally I had to ask him

what had happened on Palm Sunday. He said, "Mom, I knew you were praying, and I knew a lot of people were praying. I felt the prayers. We had to go into a house filled with Al-Qaeda. There was a terrible battle, and several Marines were killed." He said he literally felt bullets whiz by his face.

When the battle was over there were bullet holes in his clothes, but they never touched him! He said he could feel angels around him protecting him. His buddies also realized God's protection over Him and began sticking closer to him.

He came home from Iraq to California in June, 2004, due to a dislocated shoulder. He was home in time for his brother, Johns', wedding. It was so good to see him, still as handsome as ever. In just a few months he had matured about ten years (He was 26).

About six months later I was able to go to California and spend some time with him and Christie because a Christian businessman in my church gave me his frequent flyer miles. Alan is out of the service now. He has experienced severe post-traumatic stress from the war, and it has affected his marriage. But I know that the same God who protected him in Iraq, is able to heal and deliver him from the emotional and mental wounds he has. I believe God has a wonderful plan for his life, and will make him a great Spiritual warrior. And I have experienced the great power of prayer in my life.

I have talked to other mothers of soldiers who refused to watch the news or block out the fact that their son is in war. I feel differently, we are ultimately engaged in spiritual warfare in our world, and our precious sons are in the heat of the battle as soldiers. If we block out or keep too busy to pray, who will engage? We have to stay alert and sensitive to the Holy Spirit urging. I felt that God had surely spared his life!

Although it was mentally and emotionally excruciating for me, I wouldn't trade the experience for anything. I have grown by leaps and bounds spiritually and emotionally. My faith is so much stronger! I feel that I really did help my son face that terrible experience. The prayers of a mother or father availeth much. I don't know why my son survived and others didn't but I know prayer helps tremendously. It not only helps them, but helps me get through the time of having a son at war. I do believe also, that wherever God chooses to take any of our children, God will also give us the strength to go through that. The scripture verse says be vigilant, be sober.

Colleen with Alan while he was in the Marines

My Abraham/Issac Moments

I FEEL LIKE I HAVE A CALLING ON MY LIFE, TO DO GOD'S WORK, ministry: that ultimately, He is in charge of my life and He will provide. Yes, I am to do what I can, take care of home and pets, care for others as it becomes available, but not have an outside job. Unless it fits into the life I know God wants me to do for him.

When I was young, I was afraid God would want me to be a missionary in Africa. I knew I was not created to do that, yet I feared it. My wise mother told me that perhaps God wanted to see if I was willing to surrender that to Him, but that probably He would not ask that of me. So, I did lay that down. God has never asked me to be a foreign missionary, although Georgia is hot and buggy!

Much later when my firstborn was a grown marine, in Iraq in 2004, God asked me to lay him down, and I did, (That he might die in the Iraq war, he was on the front lines) and God spared his life, for a reason.

Rich, had his heart attack in Florida at Christmas in 2008. God asked me again to lay my husband down, surrender to God. I did, God did not take him.

In 2011-2012 God asked me to do a full-time large-scale women's ministry at our church, COTN. I was scared to death, but later I said "yes Lord." As of yet God has not required that of me. I am on the board of 6 women and Pastor, for that ministry.

In 2013 Fear of losing Rich and the future without him. I have laid that down too.

So far nothing God has asked of me he has required, only to surrender to see if I was willing.

God has called me to work for Him all my life! Christian wife, mom, Pastors' wife, new types of ministry. I am trying to follow & obey and trust. I've walked too far with God to turn back now. I'll follow him into eternity! It's not too far off, I can see it in the distance...

Example of Queen Esther: "If I perish, I perish." Esther 4:14-16

Cats

I DEDICATE THIS STORY ABOUT MY CATS TO MY NIECE ANDREA; WHO God used to answer my little daughter's specific prayer for a free, black and white, girl, kitten. It was in April 2000, Christina was seven. We went home to New York to be with my family. Andrea was newly married and in the first year, took in a stray cat, who in turn thanked her by giving her, right on time, a birthday present of six kittens!

Later in June we went back home and the kittens were weaned and ready to go out on their own. We were able to bring "Precious" home. She has given us years of enjoyment, entertainment, comfort, and joy. She helped Christina learn to read, as she read to the cat aloud. Precious was a very good listener and became a highly educated cat! Precious would sit with her as she did her homeschooling. She was also her confidant and playmate. Now Precious makes her home in Christina's room, she's in there all the time.

My "babies" are not the ones I gave birth to. My children, all four of them, are grown and gone except for my youngest and only daughter. She is a senior in high school. When I say my "babies" I'm referring to my cats, two of them.

The older and the fatter one was the first cat I've ever owned. My daughter and I prayed for her specifically close to a year before she was born. She had to be black and white beautiful, good and female. The other cat is small, still and not as beautiful but we never prayed for her at all. She just showed up one day years later. My daughter named her "Alice" The name doesn't fit her at all. I will probably rename her when Christina decides to fly the coop. "Mimi" I think, fits her to a tee.

Now, if my newborn grandson lived within driving distance my "babies" would take a backseat in a heartbeat, but until I can get my hands on my grandbaby and hold and cuddle and play with him, all I have is my cats. I've been waiting for my first grandchild for years.

One day, five years ago, right after my twin sister Chris had become a grandmother of twins for the first time, I was lamenting. She had called, telling me all the details of her babies. Of course, I was so excited and anxious to hear of all the news, as she was to tell me how adorable they were. At the same time, I felt the sadness as I had no baby grandchildren of my own.

I put down the phone and picked up my bigger, and only cat at the time. Precious had the most beautiful, luxurious fur coat and I hugged her, burying my face in her fur, and I said "It's not fair, Chris has two babies to love and all I have is you!" She immediately took her paw and batted my face, hissing and jumped out of my arms as if she understood exactly what I had said! After I recovered from the shock, I laughed so hard! If looks could kill I would have died; I now I'm careful what I say in her hearing.

In her older years my Precious would rather be left alone. She doesn't like to be held and petted, cuddled or hugged too much. She looks at me as if to say, "Get your own babies. You never let me have any of my own, so I don't care if you don't have any grand babies; and don't hug me either! This beautiful fur coat is for Alaskan weather not Georgia heat! I am a Yankee cat, remember? You took me from my family, my home and kidnapped me to this place that is hot enough in summer to be a doorstep to hades! So, keep me in the air-conditioning and leave me alone!" She didn't used to be so grumpy and stand offish. Looks can be deceiving. She's still so gorgeous, I tell her she's my beautiful baby anyways.

A few years ago, a kitten showed up and she was a tiny pathetic kitten, half starved. Christina started leaving water and food out for her. We could barely feed and clothe our daughter. Times were tough. We didn't need another mouth to feed however small. But she was so pitiful and kept coming back, so she adopted us as her family that she wanted. She is still small framed and loves to be near us. Always on my husband's lap or anyone who's around. At night she climbs up on top of you and sleeps. She's light as a feather and she purrs a lot, but she's going bald and the vet says it's allergies, maybe to us! Shots and drugs are all he recommended. I called another vet and I'm going back, because he's less expensive and more natural.

I have a friend, Louise, who is a cat lady. She has five cats in the house all at one time. She has even paid me to come housesit and cat sit while she's away. Talk about a cushy job! Anyway, she used to have a cat, Zack was his name, that Christina and I have always said would have made a perfect husband for precious. He was a very handsome big black and white cat, and those babies would've been so adorable. I can just imagine those little furballs. The only problem was, both cats were fixed before Louise and I became friends. I would've kept all those babies, and then my husband would've left. It's just as well, Zack up and died a year ago, and Precious would've been widowed and even more miserable than she is right now. Of course maybe her kids would've cheered her up a bit.

Christina & Colleen with "Precious" the cat.

Colleen Loran & Christine Heath

Carlisle

Carlisle came to us with his two brothers. They were all mostly black and white little fur balls, only weeks old! My teenage daughter had found them running around on the sidewalk next to the huge parking lot outside of our church, right when she and her friends came out of the youth group. These three little darlings were in great danger with all the cars coming in and out. So, they scooped them up and took them out back where there was some grass, looking in vain to find their mother!

They left them there, but all night my daughter Christina fussed and fumed and prayed for these three little kittens. The next morning instead of sleeping in (it was summer vacation), she was up bright and early and convinced her dad to take her back to the church to check on the kittens. She found them again without their mother and of course they were crying, most definitely hungry! She inquired of the church staff if they had seen their mother and then when they didn't, what was she to do? She brought the three little orphans home of course! Doesn't the Bible say we should take care of orphans?

She looked online and also called an acquaintance, who sheltered cats, and the vet to learn what she should do about taking care and feeding these little ones that were so small. The next thing I knew I was helping to feed them every three hours with a very small bottle. Christina used her own money she earned, at Chick-fil-A, to finance taking care of them. Kitten formula is not cheap. Nor was the vet to check them over; although the vet did not charge for all three cats but just one, when she saw Christina's dedication and realized she was footing the bill! My daughter took care of them around the clock except for one night-feeding, which I volunteered to do so she could go to work, and of course when she was at work. I truly felt like a grandmother!

My daughter took such good great care of them. We were really proud of her and we all learned a lot. They were so cute; one was all black, she named him Pickle. He was always getting into things. The other was Buster, the leader of the pack. He was the biggest, with a fat chubby little body and had the whitest fur, very handsome and also the most active. Then there was Carlisle. I'm not sure why she named him so. I think a friend suggested the name and it's stuck. He was very sweet, lovable and affectionate. He stole our hearts. He had one white dot on his throat. Several years earlier we had made our two-car garage into a garden room, by removing the malfunctioning double doors and framing up a wall of a screen with a screen door, so that we could use it year-round. It was a perfect room for the kittens. We fixed up an area for our new babies, containing them so they wouldn't get out. They were safe, but still had room to run, roam and play.

They wrestled each other and ran around. They were so adorable to watch. We would find them mostly in a pile sound asleep together. I had a small couch out there with a table besides, and bowl on the table. We found them a number of times all curled up in the bowl and sound asleep. Christina would go out and sit on the floor with them and they would crawl all over her. They loved her to death!

She would give them a little wash every day after they ate and check them all over. She was so good with them. She would put warm water on their feet and to this day Carlisle loves water. He sits in the laundry room sink and licks the water from the faucet.

He is so sweet. When he was younger, I would wrap him up in a soft blanket and rock him and he would go right to sleep. He's still a little love bug. He's a very calm, compassionate cat. If I can't sleep in the night, he always gets up with me while I sit in the kitchen at the table and write about him, or my life.

He has been pestering me to write about him for some time. We had found good homes for his brothers, but not for him. I'm so glad she brought the three of them home. It was such a rich experience for both of us. I just adore Carlisle and now I know my grandchildren will be well cared for!

Colleen Loran & Christine Heath

*******Christine's notes: The following Colleen wrote as a writing assignment for one of her classes.

Julie

The quaint little country church was serene as beams of sunlight shed its radiance through the colored glass windows, spreading a rainbow of color over the historic sanctuary and its antique pews. Small shellac boards arranged in an intricate design (called Wayne's coating) covered the entire ceiling and walls of the little house that was God's.

We were all in for a treat. The children were going to sing some cute choruses for the morning service. The elderly saints were smiling with anticipation and their eyes sparkled as they watched the precious youngsters assemble themselves on the left side of the pulpit by the piano. A little five-year-old girl named Julie was in the center of the group. She immediately captured the hearts of everyone in the congregation, with her radiant smile and sparkling blue eyes. Her slightly chubby cheeks were a soft pink.

As the music started Julie smiled and folded her little hands in front of her printed frock. She was singing to her heart's content swaying back and forth oblivious to everyone and everything for the duration of the songs. Her angelic face was framed with golden hair brushed to a shine and held back by a pink ribbon. The white lace collar, ruffled white petticoat, ruffed white socks and black shiny, patent-leather buckle shoes completed the picture. She was a well-proportioned child: not chubby, but not skin and bones either. Julie was a beautiful, delightful little girl. The type of child you just want to pick up and hug. She looked like a little cherub without wings, but very willing and able to take flight anyway! Her sweet innocent, carefree spirit was so enticing. Unbeknownst to her, she was the main attraction of the children's performance!

As the songs concluded the congregation broke into a thunderous and spontaneous applause. Julie very naturally obliged her audience with a smile and curtsey. That action only brought on more applause and laughter from everyone. Very pleased with herself, she filed down with the other youngsters into the front pew. They were very quiet and orderly as they seated themselves. Julie was the youngest, but conducted herself with poise imitating the conduct of the older children. They continued to act like perfect ladies and gentlemen throughout the remainder of the preliminaries; Congregational singing, offering, and prayer.

Almost as soon as the sermon began, whispering and restlessness seized Julie, She started talking to the little boy beside her, giggling and trying to smother the laughter with her little hand over her mouth. As the minutes passed Julie was getting more and more rambunctious and noisy distracting those around her. Her father quickly and quietly went up and brought her back to sit between him and her mother for the remainder of the service.

It was all done so quickly and quietly no one even noticed on the other side of the sanctuary. Julie was quiet for a moment but soon realized she was not having as much fun as she had previously had, in the company of her peers. She started whimpering and whining. Her arms folded in front of her as a big stubborn frown appeared and the pouting went on. Tears accentuated her displeasure and the next thing I knew she was on the floor under the pew! Crying more loudly and determined not to do as she was told! Stubbornness and rebellion permeated out of her little frame. She had definitely decided to make this a battle of the wills and to make her parents as miserable as she was, in the process.

Julie reminded me of the little girl in the nursery rhyme who had a little curl right in the middle of her forehead. When she was good, she was very, very good; but when she was bad, she was horrid.

I smiled and shook my head. The little angel of a moment ago, had vanished. Of course, childhood is like that. I could take in the whole scene and look at it from an objective point of view, even finding some humor, watching uninvolved, because she wasn't mine!

Colleen Loran & Christine Heath

Written by Colleen Loran In Tully, NY, On June 6, 1988

Kids Say the Funniest Things.

I was really looking forward to my trip to DC. Five days with my middle son John and my two grandchildren: Jane, age 3 1/2 and Wesley two years old. I hadn't seen them in a year! How they must've grown and changed! My youngest daughter, Chrissy would be there too. We were going to watch the children, as my daughter-in-law would be out of town at a friends' wedding, for 4 1/2 days.

Chrissy picked me up at the airport and took me to my sons' house. She had to work that day but would be able to spend the rest of the time with me. The next day Chrissy and I took care of both children all day. Then on Friday, as Chrissy had to work again, I would keep Jane. Wes would be dropped off at daycare, when his dad went to work. Jane and I had the whole day to ourselves! We took a walk, played with play dough. I put a light pink nail polish on her fingers and toes, and did her hair. Then I dressed her up in two different dresses I had bought for her and we had a photo shoot!

In the afternoon we had a garden tea party outside on the patio and read stories. She made a homemade card for her daddy for Father's Day. I had been on my feet most of the day so, as she played on the floor, I took a load off and sat down. She said "Grandma would you play with me?"

I said "sure honey, bring me what you have and I'll play with you. I don't want to get on the floor."

"Why not?" was her response.

"Well, Grandma is old and I just don't feel like getting on the floor."

"How old are you?" She asked.

"I am 61." I responded.

"That's really old isn't it?"

"Yes," I admitted with a smile on my face.

She thought for a moment and said "Grandma, how come you

don't know how to use the phone or the TV?" I laughed as I had always been technically challenged and learning how new remotes or cell phones worked was always frustrating. My husband had just given me his old (new to me) cell phone before the trip, and I was asking Christina, all the time how to do different things on it.

"Well," I said, "Grandma has to learn how to use the remote and phone because they are new to her. But I know a lot about other things."

Jane looked at me and with a childlike innocence said, "like what?"

I laughed again, "Oh, I hope I have a lot of wisdom about life." I said.

She continued to play, but it was so funny. My grandchildren are so smart, and funny and beautiful. Chrissy was allowing Jane to send texts to her mom as she knows all her letters, and little pictures. Chrissy would spell out the letters and Jane loved sending them. She also walked me through turning on the TV, to watch her favorite cartoon.

We had both of the children the rest of the weekend. We had so much fun using a sheet over the hammock to create a huge imaginary ship which went aground, and also a tent. Bubbles, water splashing in a small pool they had and listening to the birds in the backyard, we had a blast. Jane had so much fun that day I spent alone with her. She's a sweet girl and has long, fine, light brown hair. Wesley is strong and muscular; big for his age, with beautiful, almost shoulder length, blond, soft curls and blue eyes. What a charmer. He understands everything, but a little man of few words, just like his daddy was.

Colleen Loran & Christine Heath

Colleen with her grandchildren: Jane, Noah, Evelyn

God's Red and Green Lights

by Colleen Joy Loran

I never wanted to move to Georgia! I never intended to, never dreamed of it, it never even crossed my mind. It's not that I had anything against the South, or Southerners. I had no opinion whatsoever. I knew nothing of the South, except that it was hot, and I had heard somewhere that there were a lot of bugs, two facts that kept me from ever thinking about being a missionary in Africa!

I was born and raised a Yankee in upstate New York, in the beautiful Finger Lakes region, known for its deep blue lakes, waterfalls (over 1,000 of them), gorges and hills. World travelers have said that it is one of the most beautiful places in the world. I always thought so, even though I had only lived there, and in Ohio and Maryland as an adult. I had visited Florida and California.

Most of our family lives in New York, so we had no reason to move, except that Rich needed a job. He had been with a company as a Regional Manager for almost 10 years. But that company had sold, so I found myself (in my late 30's), with my new husband Rich and our 9-month-old daughter, heading to Georgia for a job interview. We looked at it as an adventure with the company paying for the trip! We were keeping an open mind, never really intending to take the job, but checking out the open door God had provided.

That was in July, 1993, and we have lived in Georgia ever since. What changed our minds? God Almighty! Rich was not impressed with the job or the company. He did not want the job. We were in the Lawrenceville area and we did not like that either...too busy, too congested, too near Atlanta. I was a country girl, used to wide open spaces, dairy farms, and beautiful landscapes.

So, we packed up and headed home. North, that's where our heart and our families were. The South was definitely not for us! But something was wrong. We both felt it as we headed home. We felt sick inside, not physically, we were fine; but in our spirits we both felt ill. We stopped the car and prayed, then started up again. We felt worse, stopped again and prayed. After going a short ways, we stopped again. We both felt awful! We didn't know what to do.

Then a thought crossed my mind. On our trip down we had both talked about doing some sightseeing. Rich had been to a city called Athens several years before, while visiting a relative of a friend and he had liked that area. "Why don't we take a few days and go there?" I asked. The company was paying for the trip and Rich had not yet told them he wasn't taking the job, so we didn't have to go home right away.

We turned around and headed for Athens. Immediate relief and peace settled in and around us. The first thing we saw was the Athens welcome center, so we stopped. The young woman attendant was warm and friendly and asked us where we were from and what had brought us to town. We simply said a job interview and she asked us if we would like a tour of the city.

She explained that a local realtor's office provided free tours, so we agreed. In no time, a gentleman named Harold Huff showed up. We learned that he was a retired Army Colonel and, more importantly, a believer in Jesus Christ. We told him what had happened to us and that we were not exactly sure why we were here. He prayed with us that God would give us wisdom, and guide and direct our path, and that we would know beyond a shadow of a doubt what we should do. He then took us on the tour.

We really liked Athens. Harold asked us if we were to move here, what kind of a home would we need and like. Well, on the way down to Georgia, just for fun, we had made a list. So, we showed him the list and he took us to several houses. Then he took us to a beautiful red brick ranch house in Oconee County. The yard was breathtakingly beautiful and immaculate. Big trees shaded the yard and there were lots of flowers. When we drove into the driveway, we felt the peace of God.

Inside was everything on our list, not one item was missing (Sometime later I realized that had forgotten a few things to write down on that list and I have often wondered if I had thought to write them down, if they would have shown up as well). We both loved the house but felt certain it would not be in our price range. It was!

What were we thinking? Rich didn't even want the job. We didn't want to move to Georgia! The more we prayed about it, the more we felt as if God wanted us to move here. What about our family being so far away? I prayed and asked God to show me a specific sign. Then out of the blue I asked what the address of this home was. I was curious that this might give us a clue. Well it gave us more than a clue. It was a confirmation (God's stamp of approval)!

1181 Daniels Bridge Road... I could not believe it. My youngest son, Daniel, was born in 1981. The number 11 turned out to be prophetic as well, but we did not understand it until years later. Daniel was accepted at the Naval Academy with a fully paid scholarship, both academically and athletically (for Lacrosse). In his senior year his Navy Lacrosse team played Syracuse for the National Championship, and it was carried by ESPN. When Daniel was on the field the ESPN announcer gave a brief bio on him and one of the things he said was that Daniel had worn the number 11 on his jersey throughout high school and college! While I had seen some of his high school games, and pictures of him in uniform, even a framed one in our home, it never registered until that moment. And he hadn't yet started high school when we bought the house! God Is so good. By the way, Syracuse won a close, exciting game, 13-12

Harold invited us to visit his church, Living Faith Fellowship, now called Church of the Nations, an Assembly of God church. The music was lively and inspiring, and the messages were very enlightening, educational and anointed. I had always wanted to go to a church like this, another answer to prayer. Well the job didn't bring us to Georgia, God did! He showed us His will by showing us where He wanted us to live and where He wanted us to go to church. We needed to know that God brought us here for reasons other than the job because, just two years after we moved a thousand miles away from everything we knew and loved, Rich was downsized out of that job! We moved into our beautiful new home in October, 1993, and we have lived here and attended Church of the Nations ever since.

Georgia turned out to be a place of tremendous healing for me, a sanctuary, and a place of wonderful teaching, restoration, spiritual growth and rest, for us. Psalm 23:2 says "He makes me lie down in green pastures. He restores my soul. He guides me in paths of righteousness for His name's sake."

He took me away from my friends and family and isolated me. I would never have chosen Georgia, but I am not God, and God knew exactly where we needed to be, and why. It was as if heading north that day when we decided Georgia was not right for us, there were all red lights; but turning around and driving to Athens, were all green lights! Isn't that how God works? He will guide and direct our path. Green lights mean green pastures!

"Then they cried out to the Lord in their trouble, and He delivered them from their distress. He led them by a straight way to a city where they could settle. Let them give thanks to the Lord for His unfailing love, and His wonderful deeds for men, for He satisfies the thirsty and fills the hungry with good things." Psalm 107: 6-9 I will give you more than you ask or think.

Our Original List (Plus the Bonus God gave us)

3-bedroom, 2-bath (spacious MB w/private bath) (Fans in all the rooms)

Garage (2 car) Fireplace w/mantle, Porch and Deck, Back yard (Fenced in)

Trees in yard (shaded house), Flowers, Nice Cabinets in Kitchen (beautiful cherry)

Laundry Room w/sink (w/cabinets for storage), Walk-in closets

Very good condition (Immaculate and well built), crown moulding

Nice kitchen (porcelain sink), granite countertops, pantry

House on road and not in a subdivision, view of horizon,

Good school district (Oconee County, one of the best in GA)

A Heart's desire Church — large, progressive, anointed and inspiring worship music and sermons, great programs for children and teens. I had grown up in small churches with little worship and less than great sermons or teaching.

"You have not because you ask not!" John 14:13-15, Luke 11:8-9

I'm Seeing Red — (From Crockpots to Cars — All in a Weeks Time!)

by Colleen Joy Loran
March, 2015

I had wanted a new crockpot, a red one! Heavy duty, with a lid that buckled shut. I had been looking for several months, just keeping my eye out. I was at Sam's Club and there was one on display that had all the features I wanted and was a good price. It even had the bonus of a small crockpot included, except it was BLACK! I asked the lady if there were any red ones. The answer was "no." I decided to get it anyway, thinking I was making way too much of the color. I thanked God, purchased it and went home.

When I got home, I went to open the box and paused. I felt an urge to pray, so, I said "Lord, you know I wanted a red crockpot.

Would you possibly make this red?" Admittedly, it was a crazy prayer. Does God care about what color your crockpot is? Probably not. He is too busy healing people, trying to prevent others from killing each other, etc.

Yet, He tells us to become like little children in our faith and that He counts the number of hairs on our head. I shrugged and opened the box. To my surprise and delight the crockpot was red! I don't know if it was red the whole time, or if God helped me to choose the right box, or if He has an acute sense of humor and decided to change it to red on the spot, as I opened it. I couldn't believe it!

Now, I know that I had just prayed and I do believe that God can do anything He wants, but that He decided to go ahead and answer that small prayer for me was HUGE to my heart! He does care about the smallest things, and He does care for me!

That very same week God answered a really big prayer for me! I had been praying for a "newer," used car for about two years. I have never had a new car and I've never cared about cars before, never even thought about them. As long as we had one that worked, was safe, clean inside, had heat, air and a radio that worked, that's all I cared about. But the last two years I really had had a desire for a nice car.

I don't know much about car makes or models, but lately I had been noticing cars and would pick out ones I liked and would mention it to my husband and asked him if he liked it too. If he wasn't around, I would inform my Heavenly Father that I liked this one or that one. I started praying specifically about "a very comfortable car, in good condition, loaded, a pretty red color, that would sit high off the road, low mileage, good on gas mileage, right price, etc." I also prayed that it would last a long time and would be our last car purchase!

Every time I would pray I would "see" a certain car in my mind, and it was RED! My husband and I had agreed that when it was the right time; we would go to a trusted, Christian friend that had a used car business. So, one day my husband asked if I'd like to go to lunch and just stop in to see what cars our friend had. As we pulled into the lot there sat the car that I had seen every time I prayed! Amazing!

It turned out to be a 2007 red and silver Chevy Trailblazer, fully loaded, sunroof, DVD player, Bose sound system, leather seats (heated), great price, etc. Our friend told us to take it for the weekend. It drove like a dream, and was so comfortable! We really did like this car but we were concerned because the mileage was a lot higher than we had wanted! So, we prayed. I felt God speak to my heart, "This is the car I showed you. It has everything you asked for and more. You need to trust me with the mileage. You said you wanted a car to last until my return. I'm coming soon!"

We bought the car. It was the only one we looked at, and we are rejoicing and praising the goodness of the Lord! "Even the very hairs on your head are all numbered." Matthew 10:30 "I tell you the truth, unless you change and become like little children you will never enter the kingdom of heaven." Matthew 18:3 "Don't worry about anything, instead pray about everything. Tell God what you need and thank Him for all He has done. Then you will experience God's peace, which exceeds anything we can ask or understand. Philippians 4:6-7 (NLT)

******Christine's notes: I found the following almost a year after Colleen's passing, in her notes and journals.*

In Case of my Death, ...I want to invite you to a celebration, not a funeral.

I know you will be hurting. I know you will miss me because I can imagine what I would go through losing you, but please come! I want you to be there.

I would like a beautiful party with all of those who cared about me to be present. To celebrate, not my death, but my eternal life with God my Father.

There were those of you who celebrated when I was born and

lived, after those first crucial months. You faithfully celebrated each birthday. You were elated when I accepted Christ, were proud the day I graduated from high school. You rejoiced on my wedding day, were thrilled when I graduated from Nursing school. We celebrated again when each of my 3 sons were born...and then my sweet little girl...

You shared my life and my joys and helped me in so many ways. Please celebrate the greatest day of my life: When I go to heaven! "For to me to live is Christ and to die is gain!"

I want music, flowers & colored balloons (helium – at my grave site to symbolize my spirit going up to meet God).

Flowers, and lots of good food. You will be hungry after all the crying and celebrating.

I want you to cry...it's good for you. Get it all out of your system. Then be happy, I AM: I AM WITH GOD! In Paradise. I have a beautiful mansion that I am decorating. I am so excited; I can hardly wait. For you see, death is like a welcome friend who beckons me to come on a long-awaited vacation to paradise! I long for death at times. Heaven is my blessed hope. I will be in the presence of God forever. Please do not grieve for me, just be ready to meet God too, so that when you die, I can see you again in heaven! Forever! We can all be together for eternity!

Overcome every circumstance, every pain, sorrow, and bitter disappointment. God alone can help you do that.

I do not fear death. It is a relief, a welcome transition from this life to the next.

Rev 21:1-7 & 22:1-5.

Songs – Debussy: *Prelude to the Afternoon of a Fawn, In His Love, Shepherd Song*

Printed in the United States
By Bookmasters